JOHNNY SHAHEED MILLER

MOTIVATED MASTERMIND

Copyright © 2023 Johnny S. Miller

All rights reserved.

Published by Johnny S. Miller.

This book or parts thereof may not be reproduced in any form, stored in any retrieval system, or transmitted in any form by any means—electronic, mechanical, photocopy, recording, or otherwise—without prior written permission of the publisher, except as provided by United States of America copyright law.

The information contained in this book and its contents is not designed to replace or take the place of any form of medical or professional advice. It is not meant to replace the need for independent medical, financial, legal, or other professional advice or services, as may be required. The content and information in this book have been provided for educational purposes only.

The content and information contained in this book have been compiled from sources deemed reliable, and it is accurate to the best of the author's knowledge, information, and belief. However, the author cannot guarantee its accuracy and validity and cannot be held liable for errors and/or omissions. Further, changes are periodically made to this book as and when needed. Where appropriate and/or necessary, you must consult a professional (including but not limited to your doctor, attorney, financial advisor, or such other professional advisor) before using any of the suggested remedies, techniques, or information in this book. Upon using the contents and information contained in this book, you agree to hold harmless the author from and against any damages, costs, and expenses, including any legal fees potentially resulting from the application of any of the information provided by this book.

This disclaimer applies to any loss, damages, or injury caused by the use and application, whether directly or indirectly, of any advice or information presented, whether for breach of contract, tort, negligence, personal injury, criminal intent, or under any other cause of action. You agree to accept all risks of using the information presented in this book.

You agree that by continuing to read this book, where appropriate and/or necessary, you shall consult a professional (including but not limited to your doctor, attorney, financial advisor, or such other advisor as needed) before using any of the suggested remedies, techniques, or information in this book.

Author: Johnny Shaheed Miller

JOHNNY SHAHEED MILLER

DEDICATION

To my father, who never stopped believing in me, thank you for your words of wisdom. Your courage and tenacity have inspired future generations. I am honored to be your son.

This one's for you!

Contents

Introduction 1
Chapter 1: Warrior Mentality 7
Chapter 2: Discipline 21
Chapter 3: Focus and Concentration 29
Chapter 4: Work Ethic 41
Chapter 5: Strategy and Positioning 53
Chapter 6: Execution 59
Chapter 7: Integrity 67
Chapter 8: Persistence 71
Chapter 9: Interdependence 77
Chapter 10: Energy, Instinct, and Intuition 83
Chapter 11: Checkmate: Endgame 93
Chapter 12: Refined Character 99
Synopsis 107
Acknowledgments 109
About The Author 123
Bibliography 127
Index 133

Introduction

It was a typical day in 2018 when I found myself in the heart of northwest Washington, DC, at the busy intersection of E St. and 22nd. After an intense workout, I was in a hurry to return home, shower, and head to work. I scanned my surroundings, noticing a bus sluggishly rolling toward me. Without giving it a second thought, I raced across the street, attempting to shave a few seconds off my trip. Little did I know, another faster-moving bus was lurking behind the one in the slow lane.

As I sprinted through the intersection, the screech of panicked brakes and the sound of tires skidding on the pavement scared the hell out of me—and then it happened. I got hit by a bus. Suddenly, I felt a tremendous impact that sent me through the air. The world spun wildly until my body crashed to the pavement a few feet from the point of impact and slid to a stop.

Dazed by what had just happened, I snapped to my feet and paused for a split second before giving the petrified driver a confident nod. I double-tapped my chest with my fist to show her I was uninjured, as if I had just performed an elaborate stunt. Her frozen expression told a different story—one of pure shock, as her stiffened body mashed into her seat with her hands gripping the steering wheel in sheer, wide-eyed terror.

Despite the accident, I was determined to shower and make it to work on time. So, without hesitation, I jogged home, ran through the water, and double-timed to my job, which was only a few minutes away. To my surprise, a colleague had witnessed the accident and approached me during a meeting to ask if I was okay. I revealed a few minor bruises but assured him that I was otherwise uninjured.

IT COULD'VE BEEN MUCH WORSE

I couldn't ruminate on the mishap because I was pressed for time and didn't want to be late to work—again. I had tunnel vision and immediately viewed the unfortunate occurrence as another obstacle to overcome. I was *on* a mission and needed to stay focused. However, recalling the incident, I instantly feel my adrenaline pumping while envisioning the fast-approaching bus just milliseconds before impact. No matter your situation, it could always be worse. Never complain; just keep pushing forward. It's about handling whatever you are dealing with. Everything else is living in the past and futile.

As someone who has achieved a few remarkable feats, I understand what it takes to unlock your full potential and break through those imaginary barriers that prevent you from confidently chasing your dreams. The wisdom you're holding at this very moment differs from anything you've ever read. It is an articulate yet comprehensive and empowering creative masterpiece that will inspire you to take charge of your life.

I don't just want to help people; I want to equip them with the mindset they need to help themselves regardless of the challenges they face. I share firsthand experiences and an empirical philosophy on human motivation to encourage readers to push through obstacles and never give up, even in the face of death. With a warrior mentality, I encourage readers to remain prepared for anything, focused, and ready to take action. Pushing forward requires tapping into your inner strength and embracing the necessity of discipline, the power of focus, the simplicity of self-reflection, and knowing your potential.

Developing resilience will cultivate the same unyielding resolve and fortitude that has empowered the strong throughout history. You will discover how discipline is the key to achieving anything. You will master the art of focus and learn to channel your energy to overcome obstacles and succeed. And that's just the beginning; this book is packed with much more!

This volume chronicles a lifetime of challenges and triumphs, including breaking a Guinness World Record, surviving a fall out of a three-story window, and numerous experiences that reveal a unique perspective for you to consider. Among other things, I am a motivational speaker, avid investor, and a successful entrepreneur managing multiple businesses. My mind has been reinforced to withstand any level of adversity, serving as a pillar of strength for myself and others.

So, if you are ready to take your life to the next level, this book is for you. I emphasize the importance of taking action rather than ephemeral words and growing through pursuing your dream. Stop making excuses, prioritize your goals, and commit to achieving them. Be accountable for your success and continue taking steps to create your vision. It is essential to face challenges with confidence and courage, recover from setbacks, and learn and grow from your experiences.

Many find themselves uninspired after being distracted by the safety and mediocrity of a job while losing sight of their dream, allowing their vision to fade into a blurred memory. It's easy to forget about your life goals, especially after establishing a daily routine while avoiding risks due to comfort or fear of failure. However, these are insignificant reasons to give up on your dreams.

Do It Anyway

Do you want to continue talking without ever making progress? Of course not. It's time to step back and ask yourself how serious you are about pursuing your aspirations. Stop procrastinating by *taking affordable steps*. Progress is a point-to-point operation, with each step advancing you closer to your destination. Achieving your goals and turning your ideas into reality takes hard work, effort, and courage. You must learn to prioritize productivity over socializing and embrace personal accountability. You can't wait for opportunities to come knocking; you must seize and create them.

You must possess a growth mindset and be open to learning from new experiences to succeed in any area of life, which may also require you to be uncomfortable and adapt. Still, it is worth the investment of time and energy.

Developing discipline before making plans is the cornerstone of building a solid foundation. Discipline and action are crucial to achieving success; plans are just dreams without those quintessential elements. Once you realize your capability and tap into the power you possess, you will be able to navigate any encounter without being deterred.

"The man who says it can't be done is generally interrupted by someone doing it."
—Elbert Hubbard[1]

It's time to tap into your inner strength, challenge yourself, prioritize your goals, and _commit_ to growth. With this book's strategies and real-world examples, you have everything you need to increase your confidence, calm your mind, sharpen your focus, and take immediate action. The journey will not be easy, but you can make it happen with discipline, focus, courage, and determination. It's time for you to believe in your abilities, embrace your true potential, and transform into the badass version of yourself you were meant to be!

---

[1] Elbert Hubbard, "The World Is Moving so Fast These Days That the Man Who Says It Can't Be Done Is Generally Interrupted by Someone Doing It," BrainyQuote, accessed September 23, 2023, https://www.brainyquote.com/quotes/elbert_hubbard_131125.

Chapter 1

WARRIOR MENTALITY

"What doesn't kill you makes you stronger."
—Friedrich Nietzsche[2]

HOW CAN A WARRIOR'S MENTALITY HELP YOU BECOME MORE SUCCESSFUL?

If you feel like life is passing you by, you are right! This chapter provides a closer, in-depth look at my thought process, personal real-life experiences, and key takeaways to keep you motivated and relentless in the face of adversity.

I was about to turn five years old, and my mother was running our bathwater, which is why I was stark naked. As my brother and I sat on the radiator near our third-story apartment's open living room window, nothing stood between us and the outside world but a thin screen, far from a safety net. I leaned on the screen in search of my friends below. My brother, who always looked out for me, snatched me back inside and told me not to lean forward. I stopped but didn't leave the window and kept guzzling my juice.

---

[2] Kayla Stoner, "Science Proves That What Doesn't Kill You Makes You Stronger," Northwestern University, October 1, 2019, https://news.northwestern.edu/stories/2019/10/science-proves-that-what-doesnt-kill-you-makes-you-stronger/.

Suddenly, I felt the facade of protection slip from my fingertips as the screen gave way—and then it happened.

I fell out the window. I felt like I was flying, but it was nothing like what I had seen on TV. I remember panicking before my body slammed to the ground, blacking out upon impact. Soon after, I woke up in the hospital without a scratch. There was no evidence that I had smacked the ground and collided with the hard orange dirt, riddled with hand-sized rocks and broken glass. I'm thankful to be alive, and I've felt an intense vibration of gratitude and optimism ever since. That experience, and a few others, forever changed me and helped shape the man I am today. I have made it through so much that my mind has become strong enough to handle anything. Nothing can hurt me or stand in my way as long as I continue to choose to grow from my experiences and fight forward.

YOU ARE A WARRIOR! SH*T HAPPENS – LEARN FROM IT!

Everything revolves around this single thought:

No matter what, I will keep pushing. Failure is not an option, and regardless of unforeseen obstacles, I will keep fighting and never give up, even in the face of death.

I have a small circle of friends and family. One thing they would unanimously say about me is that I am a problem solver. I enjoy the challenge of figuring things out because for every problem presented, there is a solution awaiting discovery. Several people, none more significant than my father, have told me that I am the smartest person they know, which is an enormous compliment.

While this acclamation is incomprehensible, receiving it has only intensified my discipline and sharpened my focus, which are the subjects of the two ensuing chapters. This is my first literary work of this type; while reading it, you may experience sudden bursts of energy, fresh ideas, and different perspectives to keep you engaged and inspired.

HOW TO TAKE ADVANTAGE OF OPPORTUNITY?

> "Excuses will always be there for you; opportunity won't."
> —Unknown[3]

They say opportunity only knocks once, but sometimes it never does. In those instances, you must create one. You are the architect of your reality. When you understand your power, you will embrace challenges with confidence. *Scire te ipsum*, Latin for "Know yourself," is a characteristic of consciousness that may prove advantageous when choosing your path. You have the power to create opportunities when they do not otherwise exist.

USE YOUR TIME WISELY

> "Work like there is someone working twenty-four hours a day to take it from you."
> —Mark Cuban[4]

You know exactly what areas you are wasting time on and which areas you need to improve, right? There's nothing wrong with taking a break but understand that progress requires consistency. If you are scrolling through social media, just shooting the breeze, or overthinking instead of taking action, you aren't making progress. You must take advantage of those instances when you feel the most motivated, capable, and focused, which is when you are at your best; don't waste these moments.

---

[3] Heather, "Excuses Will Always Be There for You. Opportunity Won't," Mindset Made Better, Novemebr 28, 2022, accessed September 23, 2023, https://mindsetmadebetter.com/2022/11/excuses-will-always-be-there-for-you-opportunity-wont/.

[4] Mark Cuban, "Work Like There Is Someone Working Twenty-Four Hours a Day to Take It All Away from You," Quotefancy, accessed September 23, 2023, https://quotefancy.com/quote/1151819/Mark-Cuban-Work-like-there-is-someone-working-twenty-four-hours-a-day-to-take-it-all-away.

Though your community and support system are vital for balance and a healthy social life, prevent people from getting in your head. I only take advice from those who practice what they preach. I don't know anyone else pursuing the same path as me, and I don't need a mentor. I have a vision and will continue to learn, follow my gut, and take action, regardless of what occurs.

Your instincts should be trusted completely. You are made from your experiences and how you respond to them, mentally and intellectually. Some people are made to be tougher, stronger, and more relentless than others. Everybody's mission is different, but we were all created to be warriors in some capacity. There is nothing wrong with crying, but you need to stay on your hardcore killer sh*t—tears or not.

With that said, you may not want to be tough all the time, but preparation is key. Be sure you are prepared both mentally and physically for anything. For example, how would you foil the attack if somebody invaded your home tonight and attempted to harm you or one of your loved ones? Live in peace but be prepared to respond if faced with the worst-case scenario.

> "It's better to be a warrior in a garden than a gardener in a war."
> —Bruce Lee[5]

Let the emotions out, embrace the pain, and keep one foot on the gas and your finger on the trigger.

Life is not a game; it's war! Nobody cares about your tears. There is absolutely nothing wrong with having emotions. I encourage you to understand the relationship between your thoughts, sentiments, and actions; however, when taking action, you must put your feelings on the shelf until you have finished taking care of business.

---

[5] Moneer Marouf, "Obsidian Studio Announces Edyn, an Action Adventure Game Taking Place in a Vibrant Immersive World," EIN Presswire, February 7, 2022., https://www.einnews.com/pr_news/562507694/obsidian-studio-announces-edyn-an-action-adventure-game-taking-place-in-a-vibrant-immersive-world.

Given the current mindset of the world, especially the younger generations, we need to increase our mental fortitude, focus, and willpower. Instead of a lighter load, we should look for greater strength to carry that load, and instead of praying for that strength, we should tap into the strength we already have.

How Strong is Your Mind?

After leaving Saudi Arabia several years ago, where the average temperature during the summer months exceeds a hundred degrees in the shade, I returned to Okinawa, Japan, with a mutant-like characteristic triggered by cold temperatures. I suffered from dermographism urticaria (an illness caused by the skin releasing histamine in the absence of allergens) that caused me to break out in severe itchy hives on any area of my skin exposed to temperatures south of 69 degrees.

In the wake of dealing with the frustration of the irritating skin condition for a few years, I'd had enough and decided to fight back and end the torment. One freezing evening, after leaving the gym and drenched in sweat, I stood outside in the snow for a few hours, wearing only a wet tank top, enduring the bone-chilling temperature. It was a test of mind over matter until the cutaneous plague surrendered. Subsequently, I never experienced another episode.

You don't need advice if you are willing to tap into your higher self. You need to figure out what you're made of. You may need a reminder, but don't rely on anyone to help you out of your situation. Therein lies the problem. Everybody keeps looking out and looking up instead of looking within. You were meant to be great! You are great! Love yourself, stay motivated, and trust your ability to figure things out.

Who Are You?

That is the purpose of self-reflection and self-awareness. Sit and look inward. See what you are capable of, what you desire, and what motivates and inspires you. Who are you? You can't say you don't know because that doesn't require any thought. You can't excuse yourself from answering because that isn't the action of a responsible adult. You are a warrior!

Your block in life is not accepting the calling of who you know you are. This could be the result of society's intentional psychological manipulation convincing you to seek the comfort offered by denial of purpose, wandering aimlessly without the compass of accountability that comes with selecting a targeted goal or destination. The truth is, your mind never stops, and you will constantly struggle with feeling like you are living a different life than your purpose until you decide to do something about it. Soul-searching requires isolation and deep thought. If you think otherwise, you're probably still soul-searching. And while you take time to look inside and sort through your confusion, know that you are stronger than any distraction or temptation.

Most will talk and tell you their thoughts, plans, hopes, and dreams but never do anything with their ideas. Most people don't execute and rely on an infinite list of irrefutable excuses to support their lack of ambition. Look at your spouse, family member, or close friend, or better yet, take a good look in the mirror. How is that invention coming along? Have you applied to Shark Tank yet? Are you still thinking about crowdfunding? You have a great idea and a bulletproof plan but can't find time to focus on your idea and nothing else because life keeps getting in the way, right? I understand, trust me, I get it, but get this: all of your excuses are bullsh*t. There's always a way; you must find it!

WHAT ARE YOU AFRAID OF?

Great ideas are a dime a dozen, but developing a focused plan and consistently working towards achieving whatever you set your sights on takes unyielding willpower and a clearly defined motive. Don't lose sight of your 'Why.' Make your mind bully your body to eliminate distractions and take action. Imagine awakening early for work refreshed and deciding to check social media (indeed, you have a few likes and comments) to browse the newsfeeds to get a taste of what is waiting idly for you, and then—*bam*. Without even realizing it, you are hooked and passing the morning away.

TICK-TOCK

Time flies by. Days seem like hours. You're not making progress because you're just chilling. Who needs personal improvement, growth, financial freedom, or to maximize time when you already have a steady nine-to-five? You are comfortable, so your goals and ambitions can go unexplored, untapped, and untouched because your great ideas are known. You previously told everybody what you are working on, so you have already received accolades for your brilliance. That little dopamine high (the neurotransmitter responsible for positive feelings of reward and motivation) you receive when discussing your plans is not yours or real. It's like getting paid before you do the work. Do you know how it feels to get hard-earned money? When you get paid, it feels like you deserve it, right? You cherish it and spend it wisely because of the effort it took to create it. Your bills and expenses almost have to pry it from your tightly clinched fingers. On the other hand, when it comes too quickly, you don't appreciate it because you can print more by making another false promise of all the things you will do that will never get done. Conversely, when taking care of business, you become a person of increased character and work ethic. I swear it's true. Action requires no words. Talk is cheap. Only Respect Action!

Maybe you are afraid of failure or apprehensive because of the thought of your ideas being rejected or unappreciated. Could it be that you fear success, for that comes with navigating foreign territory; you will have to learn or inherit too many daunting tasks, which is unattractive because your plate is already full? Mediocrity is safe, and just getting by is, unfortunately, being normalized. Well, guess what? Like I said previously, none of your excuses are good enough if you are serious about your goals.

So first, take a second, pry yourself away from repetitive stimuli, renounce vacillation, and ask yourself: *How bad do I want this?* Are you satisfied with your current life circumstances, or are you willing to go hard, grind it out, and make impactful changes? Stop procrastinating! Today is yesterday's tomorrow. Start small, start now, or you never will.

As I reflect on the periods of my life when I arrived at crossroads in search of direction, I had to make some tough decisions. Everything I needed to do became apparent after isolating myself to clear my head and focus on what I needed to accomplish. I decided what mattered to me the most, determined if I had the means to obtain it (if not, I generated that means), focused, and committed.

"Winning isn't everything, but wanting to win is."
—Vince Lombardi[6]

Remember, no matter how hard it gets, you must continue to fight. You can handle it. Face it and embrace it! That's what true courage feels like. Have confidence in your ability to figure things out, take the pain, bounce back, and learn. Push past the points of fear and failure. If you are going to fail, it is better to fail fast and learn from those mistakes. Action eliminates fear. If you are willing to devote your time to trying new things, you may consequently fail often in the process, but this is powerful; you only have to be right once, so the more frequently you get results, the higher your likelihood of reaching your goal. Professional athletes, presidents, astronauts, and inventors all had one thing in common: they kept fighting while becoming legendary and making history.

A Man with Two Minds

My purpose is to motivate, inspire, and change lives. Dreams only come true if you make them by applying consistent and focused effort. I have witnessed several talented people attempt to juggle a multitude of ideas simultaneously, ultimately making no progress due to their inability to clearly define priorities and align their thoughts and actions with an efficient growth strategy. It's not because they didn't have ideas; collectively, they had thousands to choose from, but insanity could also

---

[6] Meet Shah, "Winning Isn't Everything, but Wanting to Win Is," Setquotes, August 14, 2022, https://www.setquotes.com/winning-isnt-everything-but-wanting-to-win-is/.

be defined as *a man with two minds*. Pick one. Be serious about whatever you're working on; focus on that and nothing else. Decide, commit—that's it! It's not about talking. It's about believing in yourself, taking action, and giving your all.

If you lack confidence and are unwilling to trust your abilities due to limiting beliefs resulting from traumatic past experiences, you can use your actions to change your thoughts. A behavioral psychologist might use a similar technique, attempting to use thoughts to change someone's actions.

I have listened to several stagnant people about pursuing their goals, and there is one thing they all have in common: they have not committed. Establishing a clear, unyielding resolve before engaging in any activity will help you stay the course, especially when things get tough or inevitably do not go as planned.

I Knew the Job was Dangerous when I Took It

I remember experiencing my first mortar attack. It all happened so fast. I was in southern Iraq at Camp Adder (Tallil Air Base) and was honored to be accompanied by Master Chief Petty Officer Timothy Sheridan, Ret. U.S. Navy. It was a quiet day. We had just finished eating lunch and returning to resume operations when several mortars whizzed past us overhead. I had no idea what was going on. I recall being surrounded by a cacophony of explosions that caused the earth to tremble beneath our feet, immediately catching our attention. I also noticed a few artillery shells detonated in the distance, about fifty to a hundred meters north. And before we could respond, there were a few explosions twenty to thirty meters to our left, over the Hesco barriers that enveloped the Romanian camp.

My first thought was to get my guys to safety. We reacted by sprinting toward our shop, thirty meters east, and I screamed, "Get your sh*t on!"—referring to their protective vest and helmet. Once everyone snatched their gear, which took about half a second, I told them to hop in the Suburban, and we headed straight for the hardened aircraft hangar close to the airport because I knew everyone would be protected from incoming rounds. I would have rather died than have let something happen to one of my guys on my watch.

Was it scary? A little, but there were lives at stake. I was aware of the imminent danger and the possibility of death, but I was motivated to act and quickly responded. That day, Tim referred to me as their "fearless warrior!" What a great compliment from someone who stared death in the face several times, but I could not accept the accolade. I felt fear, but I did not let that stop me. Before going to war, I decided that regardless of any degree of adversity, I would rather die fighting than live in fear, and my courage answered the call to protect my team. It was a proud moment for us all.

Indecisiveness, fear of failure, doubt, and procrastination have killed more dreams than failure ever will. When you *decide*, the rest is easy. It comes down to what you want to do and how badly you want it.

On December 17, 2022, I officially became the Guinness World Record holder for the most weight lifted by dumbbell curls in one minute. With one arm, I curled sixty-two reps for a combined total of 2,492.40 pounds. The mere mention of the record-breaking attempt takes me back to the outset of preparation. I experienced a few setbacks along my journey, but giving up never crossed my mind. While deployed to northern Kuwait in 2015, I worked at least twelve hours a day, every day, and trained incessantly.

Around two in the morning, I was killing an arm workout while playing "Lyrical Exercise" by Jay-Z. It was my last set; I turned my music up and hit the weights with Mike Tyson-like tenacity—and then it happened. While performing a set of bicep preacher curls, with 225 pounds plus the weight of the easy curl bar, I tore my left bicep. It felt like a hot, thick rubber band snapped between my elbow and bicep, which slid up my arm, causing an intense burning sensation. The first step of my recovery plan was the RICE method, which includes rest, ice, compression, and elevation.

I continued to train daily and adjusted my regimen to include light to moderate weight when performing any exercises that required my biceps to engage. And then it happened—again. Seven years later, while preparing for an unrelated world record for which I still await Guinness approval, I tore my other bicep, performing farmer's carries while jogging with 120-pound dumbbells in each hand. I did not have the weights in an optimal position, which resulted in injury, causing me to straighten my arms and drop the weight. I kept plowing away, seeking relief from the *ICE* method—because there was not much rest. After breaking the record, a great friend of mine, Calvin Watford, asked, "Do you realize you did this with two torn biceps?" I paused before replying, "I never thought about it." He laughed and said, "I guess that's why you are the world record holder."

We experienced a mishap while filming the initial official record-breaking attempt. Video evidence is required to verify that all attempts are performed based on strict guidelines provided by the Guinness World Records administration before accepting applications from future record applicants. After successfully breaking the record once, curling sixty-three reps in one minute (2,532.6 pounds), we began to celebrate, but that moment was short-lived. While gathering all the signatures and reviewing the captured footage, we discovered that somebody forgot to hit the record button, likely due to all the excitement. The event organizer, Brian Cavanaugh, was pissed, but we immediately adjusted, gathering in our recently rehearsed positions. And the rest is history. We did it. Now, it's time to crush another one!

If you have a clear vision, continue to pursue it until it comes to fruition. Don't let anything stand in your way. Not everybody is going to be motivated and encouraged. Most people want the comfort a steady paycheck provides, and very few have a vision for their future. Some people do not believe in themselves *yet*, so due to life circumstances and attrition, they don't pursue their goals, or give up in the process. You are different, and there is a reason you are reading this book. Do not become one of the many; be one of the few warriors who give it everything. Make a conscious decision to commit and take what you want. That is the only way to ensure the highest rate of success.

"Our greatest weakness lies in giving up. The most certain way to succeed is always to try just one more time."
—Thomas Edison[7]

It comes down to one thing: your mindset. It is not about who you know—connections can help you find a shorter, more direct route, but so can your research and strategic thinking. Your idea doesn't have to be world-changing, and you don't require as much funding as you think to get started. Several start-ups have launched from garages or street corners that have penetrated their markets, making their creators famous. You will always succeed if you are hyper-focused, consistent, and willing to work diligently. Persistence requires grit, determination, and occasional sacrifices. Ultimately, it comes down to who you are and what you are willing to fight for.

Make a decision. Again, once you decide, the rest is easy. If you never decide that you are going to make it happen no matter what, you will float aimlessly. When you decide that nothing will stand in your way, nothing will!

Have you ever wished you had decided what you really wanted to do and didn't stop until you got it done? Regrets. We must learn to live with them, right? No. That's just a trivial colloquialism sold to pacify you and alleviate your pain while delaying your acceptance of failure and missed opportunities. Truthfully, you do not have to learn to live with regrets; not the guilt of not giving it your all. In life, things happen, but your effort is controllable. Remember: Your willingness determines your effort, but your effort determines your performance.

I prefer productivity over running my mouth, with an emphasis on personal accountability. I'm always willing to push myself, no matter what. We are so

---

[7] Thomas Edison, "Our Greatest Weakness Lies in Giving up. The Most Certain Way to Succeed Is Always to Try Just One More Time," BrainyQuote, accessed September 23, 2023, https://www.brainyquote.com/quotes/thomas_a_edison_149049.

blessed to have the opportunity to shape our lives into our desired futures. Many people in the world don't have that option. You still must make the most of what you are presented with, even if you must change everything. There is always a way to progress once you decide to keep pushing, regardless of what occurs. There are 86,400 seconds in a day. Divided by three, that is 28,800. Think about it. If you work eight hours and sleep eight hours, you still have about thirty thousand seconds of free time to accomplish anything. Just decide and commit. That's it.

Now that we've established the 'how' and the 'why,' consider a few more questions: What's your current mindset? Do you have a growth mindset? Can you intelligibly grasp and manipulate information and use it to improve in all areas of life? Or is your perception myopic or nearsighted? Regardless of your perspective, I want you to understand and embrace that you have the power to accomplish anything. When you realize this, you become dangerous because you refuse to quit. You will not stop at "*no*" or "*sorry*." It will take a lot more to knock you off your warpath.

Open your mind to the idea that I'm right. Countless others have harnessed the power of their minds, focused on what they wanted, and changed lives. Remain encouraged. Live every moment and enjoy your time figuring it all out. Now, before you jump straight in, begin to brainstorm, write down all your ideas step-by-step, and transcribe that information into the blueprint of your life; there are additional tenets that require clarification, which the ensuing chapters will provide.

MOVING AHEAD

In this chapter, you decided to push yourself no matter what. With tunnel vision and hyperfocus, you can continue to break through barriers rather than running in circles. The key to maintaining this momentum is *discipline*.

CHAPTER 2

DISCIPLINE

"You will never find time for anything. If you want time, you must make it."

—Charles Buxton[8]

HOW CAN DISCIPLINE AND SHORT-TERM SACRIFICES INCREASE YOUR CHANCES OF LONG-TERM SUCCESS?

Now that we have established a solid foundation, let's discuss what separates talkers from doers. Behind the scenes on a movie set in Hollywood, everything is well planned and rehearsed before filming starts.

Everyone knows their lines, so there isn't much to discuss. There are defined roles with specific responsibilities, even a time limit for all aspects of production. We have the perfect venue, big-name actors, a director, producers, a budget, investors, distribution, marketing and advertising, camera crew, special effects, lighting, props, stuntmen, body doubles, and a great soundtrack with unreleased music from top A-list artists. Even the

---

[8] Charles Buxton, "You Will Never Find Time for Anything. If You Want Time You Must Make It," BrainyQuote, accessed September 23, 2023 https://www.brainyquote.com/quotes/charles_buxton_104418.

best name for a film ever thought of—but none of that makes a movie without action!

> "There are only two days in the year that nothing can be done. One is called yesterday, and the other is called tomorrow."
> —Dalai Lama[9]

NO EXCUSES

Relentlessly pursuing your dreams and taking consistent action requires discipline. It is easy to begin anything. You can wake up every morning with thoughts of things that would be great to accomplish. That is effortless. But to start and finish takes someone willing to act in a particular manner with an established continuum of task orientation and execution, irrespective of external factors beyond our control. It is textbook discipline to shut up and grind! Life will happen. Embrace that fact; use your experiences as a cornerstone and catalyst for change and growth.

> "There are no secrets to success. It is the result of preparation, hard work, and learning from failure."
> —Colin Powell[10]

What is discipline? Discipline is a commitment to consistently act in a particular manner established to help you reach your primary objective.

---

[9] Dalai Lama, "There Are Only Two Days in the Year That Nothing Can Be Done. One Is Called Yesterday and the Other Is Called Tomorrow," Minimalist Quotes, accessed September 23, 2023, https://minimalistquotes.com/dalai-lama-quote-8442/.

[10] Pamela Leibowitz, ""There Are No Secrets to Success. It Is the Result of Preparation, Hard Work, and Learning from Failure."- Colin Powell," Suffolk Center for Speech, accessed September 23, 2023, https://www.lispeech.com/there-are-no-secrets-to-success-it-is-the-result-of-preparation-hard-work-and-learning-from-failure-colin-powell/.

Indeed, actions speak louder than words. Nobody cares what you are talking about. They only care about what you are doing. The results speak for themselves. We all know those talkers—they tell the same story but never do anything. This only delays progress. I will show you how to avoid going in five directions simultaneously. I will teach you how to capitalize on your motivation by maximizing your level of discipline.

TALK LESS AND <u>DO</u> MORE

My dad told me, "Most people live and die with a good idea!" Don't become another statistic. You are brilliant, and everybody knows it, but you may not feel supported. Perhaps the people who know you best think you are incapable of change and assume you will keep talking but do nothing. Whatever; who cares; kill all excuses! Do it anyway. Make your mind bully your body. Those ideas in your head are useless until you shut up and use your discipline to put those plans on paper and force those ideas to convert to action. Once you get them down, categorize everything so the information makes sense at a glance and put it all on a task timeline. Next, cross-reference that timeline with a to-do list and set a completion date.

We just removed the excuse of not knowing how. It's time! Jump on top of that business plan, set a completion date, and stick to it, no matter what. Determine what areas you need assistance in and find those inventive minds who can help you propel toward your goal. Take affordable steps. Even with a tight budget, a freelancer can assist you with your advertising, graphics, search-engine-optimized content, or whatever you need. Just get started now, and if you need help, refer to this book. Use the table of contents as a reference or reminder.

It is healthy to brainstorm, create, and let your mind run wild, but when it comes to business and being productive, it is only about getting it done. You have the power to make your mind bully your body to do what you have to do. Capture the moment. Feel that rush of energy without procrastinating. Give it all you've got, and don't get distracted. It is crucial to concentrate, which requires laser-like focus. Once you are in your zone, success can become routine. Healthy habits and daily schedules that you follow no matter what can ensure you stay on track. Enjoy yourself but set boundaries so you can gauge how you're performing and where to adjust.

I have a confession. I'm an ordinary person, but do you know what's extraordinary? My mindset, discipline, and laser-like focus. Action, consistency, and accountability are everything. Want a better body? Eat healthy, reduce calories, and work out. Want more money in your savings or money market account? Stop spending so much on unnecessary products and invest (slowly). Bored, try searching for new hobbies. Has it been a while since you had a date? What about personal interaction? Want a better life? Cut off those negative people you so comfortably surround yourself with. There's always a way if you are willing to break out of your comfort zone and take the necessary steps.

I operate from a daily schedule. I go to sleep with clear objectives if I am fortunate enough to wake up each morning. I begin each day with a routine and follow it no matter what.

Master Self-Control

> "Success is to be measured not so much by the position that one has reached in life as by the obstacles which he has overcome while trying to succeed."
> —Booker T. Washington[11]

I lost my mother at the end of 2019. I was off work from state department operations, and it was Monday, aka Universal Chest Day. I started training outside the gym on Mondays but had a thousand push-ups to do. A few moments before I started getting ready, I got the call. I could tell what had happened by the caller's first words. Her dejected tone said it

---

[11] Booker T. Washington, "Success Is to Be Measured Not so Much by the Position That One Has Reached in Life as by the Obstacles Which He Has Overcome," BrainyQuote, accessed September 23, 2023, https://www.brainyquote.com/quotes/booker_t_washington_107996.

all. She asked me if I was sitting down, and after I responded, she told me that my mother had passed away.

It was unexpected and completely knocked the wind out of me. I remember hanging up the phone and taking a deep breath in preparation for the tears to rush to my eyes. But I couldn't cry. At that moment, I heard my mother say, "What's crying going to do? It's not going to bring me back. You're still going to do those push-ups!" And at that moment, I felt her presence and strength.

TIME REMAINS LIMITED, WHILE EXCUSES ARE IN ABUNDANCE

Instead of looking for excuses to quit, look for reasons to fight and keep going. To master yourself, you must first master self-control. Create a plan and force yourself to stick to it while making immediate adjustments whenever necessary. Keep progressing. It may start as challenging because it is foreign. You have no idea what to expect, so you don't know how to prepare and probably assume the worst out of fear. Trust me, I know. But this default thinking pattern is just your mind's way of trying to protect you from re-experiencing pain in any form. Learn to silence those crippling voices because they have no idea who you are or what you are capable of. Self-control is self-mastery.

Self-control is always necessary; you can't just fly off the handle and explode without expecting a commensurate response. For instance, when communicating, speak your mind and express yourself, but remember: Anger is a sign of stupidity. It is a gateway to sickness and slow death. However, if you can systematically provoke and enrage your opponents, they will become frustrated and respond out of character.

I'm not advising you to add this method to your repertoire. However, when you employ this tactic skillfully, it can be a powerful weapon. Never lose control. You should focus on developing the discipline necessary to pursue your vision. Sometimes you just won't feel like doing anything because it may appear to take away from your fun and consume too much of your time. You may also wonder if the investment of time and energy will be worth the sacrifice. I experience similar thoughts while evaluating opportunity costs and deciding what to focus on. You will always grow from a learning experience. When you think about it, if you don't want to do something, you will take your time and half-ass it, so it will never reflect your full potential. So, you can't say that you tried if you only give it a half-assed effort. But here is the answer: It is definitely worth it, especially if it's something you love or are serious about.

This next thought will sound like an infomercial, but here goes. By investing a few minutes a day in any particular area of improvement, you will begin to develop a healthy habit within a few weeks. After researching the best methods of healthy habit development, I know what works for me. The more I do something, the more it becomes instinctive, and I begin to look forward to doing it, especially after noticing the benefits, which makes the habit stick.

Remember why you started. Those short-term goals you learned about long ago are the milestones that will keep you pushing. For instance, if your aim is to save $200,000, don't wait to celebrate until you reach your final goal. Celebrate each thousand. Success is a path, not a destination.

For instance, let's say you were eating right because you wanted to drop ten pounds in thirty days, which is super easy, right? After the first four days, you gained three pounds. Wait—what happened? You were eating clean but consuming too many calories, so you were not losing weight, and felt defeated because you were doing everything right but still missed your target. But where was the flaw?

Since you were eating too many calories, you decided to reduce your daily caloric intake by a hundred calories by removing cheese from your afternoon and evening salads. You also chose to increase your water intake and pay closer attention to sodium because sodium holds water, among other things. You also increased your protein intake because it requires more energy to process protein. And guess what? You dropped more weight than you anticipated. You are down six pounds in the first seven days, and now you are considering implementing several types of cardio because you see your plan working.

> **Key Takeaway:** Discipline with noticeable benefits will help ensure consistency.

As you maintain constant effort while taking affordable steps, keeping your goals in mind will keep you moving in the right direction. It seems simple, and it is. It is also easy to get distracted and start doing something irrelevant that has nothing to do with your goal but everything to do with what you are most comfortable doing. For instance, you can use free marketing tools like social media, blog posts, web articles, and video sharing services to satisfy algorithm requirements by providing search-engine-optimized content. At some point, you may post once or twice a day, engage with your followers, and find yourself distracted while hooked into watching entertaining shorts and reels. This can become comfortable and addictive and even feel like progress. It's not. Don't forget about the main goal.

Using checklists and measurable metrics is vital to ensure you are making progress. Stick to the script until you hit your primary objective. Maintain your level of discipline, keep your motivated state of mind, and stay focused.

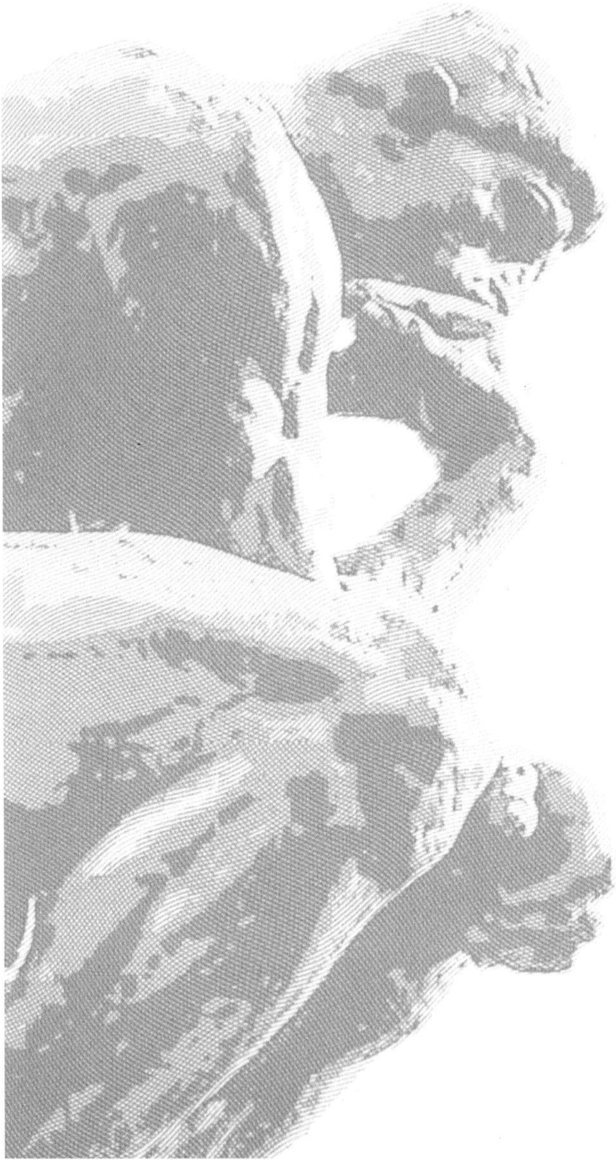

Chapter 3

FOCUS AND CONCENTRATION

"To do two things at once is to do neither."
—Publius Syrus[12]

HOW CAN MANAGING DISTRACTIONS AND PRIORITIZING TASKS HELP YOU STAY COMMITTED TO YOUR GOALS?

The following is a cringeworthy recap of an incident during my childhood in Washington, DC. I was five years old. It was a scorching summer day, approximately 95 degrees. As I recall, there were about twelve of us in total. The older kids, esteemed as the leaders and decision-makers, decided that we were going to the creek, located a little farther than a mile away in a park by the name of Oxen Run. It was difficult to navigate because we had to cross two busy highways—Southern Avenue, which separates DC from Maryland, and Suitland Parkway, before traveling through a path that led us directly to the forest-covered park.

Upon arrival, I was hungry, as usual. Families were cooking, and the aroma of savory food ready to eat intensified my hunger pangs. I was immediately captivated by the shallow, warm, flowing water containing slippery rocks perfect for throwing. This was my first time in the water;

---

[12] Bodhipaksa, "Publilius Syrus, "To Do Two Things at Once Is to Do Neither"," Wildmind, February 23, 2009, https://www.wildmind.org/blogs/quote-of-the-month/publilius-syrus.

swimming was a foreign concept. I attempted to skip rocks in the creek for about two or three minutes when I instinctually looked up in search of familiar faces, and all the kids had disappeared. I was suddenly surrounded by strangers. but I didn't panic because I knew the way home. Tired from the long walk through the woods and still hungry, I spotted my original group making their way up the creek on the left side of the water, walking against the current in a section shielded from the sun; it looked like fun. I screamed, "Hey, wait up! Here I come!"

A few of the older kids who were trying to catch up to the slow-moving group about thirty yards ahead repeatedly tried to persuade me not to tag along, but I brushed them off. I didn't want to be left out, so I removed my shoes and decided to proceed. The task of moving up alongside the creek became exceedingly difficult. We had to maintain a position of at least a forty-five-degree angled plank as we walked for a few hundred yards against the endless gray wall of enormous dusty rocks held in place by what appeared to be some sort of fence. This challenge would soon pale in comparison to what lay ahead. I had no idea that I was about to be tested beyond measure.

It appeared that we caught up to the older kids, but in hindsight, they must've slowed down to wait for us and keep us safe. I was exhausted, sweaty, and stumbling, partly because I was not wearing shoes. Disoriented and ready to pass out, I recall being surrounded by kids closer to my age who convinced me not to sit down. To my surprise, we ran out of shade a few minutes later, and it was suddenly a lot hotter than I remembered. I grew increasingly thirsty and was determined to rest, but whenever I tried to take a break, somebody would pull me up to prevent me from resting. This was very frustrating because I didn't understand why and felt like I needed a nap.

I decided to sit down anyway, collapsing all my weight on the fence—and then it happened. I was met with the unwelcoming resistance of a few hundred bees. They swarmed and attacked me all over. They stung my eyelids, lips, mouth, arms, hands, and neck. Everybody rushed to save me, swatting at bees, plucking the residuals of their twitching abdomens from my face. The mission quickly evolved to get me to safety, but we had about thirty yards to go, which is where I would stumble across what was then my greatest challenge.

Once we made it to the end of the infinite fence, a calm pool of water emptied into the creek. I was scared of the water because I couldn't distinguish the path I needed to walk from the dark, murky green water. I proceeded anyway, with everyone shouting in the background. When I got across the first section of the wall, there was a drop of about two feet. This is where the calm body of water rushed like a small downward waterfall to create the creek. I faced the challenge of stepping down from the wall onto the most slippery surface known to man. It was like walking on oily ice. I imagined I would die if I fell into the water and felt a sense of fear like never before. The pain I experienced from the recent attack was incomprehensible, but I needed to focus, not on the pain and anxiety from the burning on my swollen and throbbing face, but on not falling into the deep end of where the creek met the life-threatening waterfall.

I just wanted to fast-forward the day and escape my situation, but I couldn't think about that. It was hard to see because my eyes were burning and swelling shut. I decided to focus all my attention on not falling into the water. I had no other choice but to concentrate. Taking my first step, I slipped and almost fell into the creek. I was forced to grab the wall while in search of solid footing. The rushing water across my bare feet only contributed to my lack of balance and instability. I tried to hold on to the ground while sliding in slow motion across the waterfall. I patiently navigated to the other side, bracing for that slippery, wet, mossy walkway to send me plunging cartoon-style into the water. I didn't fall. Everyone made it safely, and I recovered within a day or so.

Key Takeaway: When facing significant challenges, even those with seemingly insurmountable odds, focus like your life is on the line, and you will be amazed by what you can accomplish.

Hopefully, by this point, you feel like a new person or a refreshed, reinvigorated, refined, and more motivated version of your true self. To my most recent point, our potential is practically and intellectually unlimited. However, this can be stifled by short-sightedness, lack of ambition, negative influences, or low self-esteem, all of which can be fixed by doing more. Let me explain.

Confidence comes from doing—This is your verified proof of capability, and I want you to continuously add more items to your arsenal after reflecting upon your accomplishments. If you have never failed, you have never tried. The more you practice, the better you will become, even with an extensive history of unsuccessful attempts. If you keep pushing, you will grow in unimaginable aspects that are only comprehensible through hindsight and self-reflection, which will also dramatically improve how you feel about yourself, especially in the specific area of concentration. Determination is required to continue to push beyond setbacks and disappointment. Stay relentless; don't let up!

REAL-WORLD APPLICATION

Let's talk about how this shows up in your day-to-day life. What does all this motivation and certainty look like? We have already established that nothing is going to stop us. Your willingness to do whatever it takes is exceptionally high. You carved out small chunks of time from your busy schedule. You decided to wake up a few minutes early to work out three days a week, cut your lunch break short to devote time to conduct research and review your to-do list, and even scheduled time to take calls on your way home from work. You are doing several seemingly small but significant things to boost your productivity. But in a few weeks, the unexpected happens: your car breaks down, your employer cuts your hours, and your paramour decides it's best to separate and see other people.

CRISIS AVERTED

This is the end of the world, right? Hell no! Nothing is, and nothing ever will be. You decide to quickly pivot, cut your spending, and negotiate a deal to catch a ride with one of your neighbors, which will also help them with gas expenses while you figure out which account you will pull the funds from. And as you think about it, you are glad you are single because you can use the time to focus on your new business and catch up with family and friends.

I like how you adjusted on the fly, stayed focused, and kept moving. That is what the right mindset, discipline, and focus allow you to do. Life will happen. Anticipate the unexpected and embrace those instances as growth opportunities. Now, let's open the conversation to applying focus. Laser-like focus is defined as being without distraction.

Ever heard of attention engineering? These concepts are applied to engage and confuse users and customers for a prolonged duration to collect information and maximize revenue generation. For instance, let's look at how these concepts are applied at casinos. There are no windows, so you have no idea what time of day it is. All you hear are happy sounds indicative of winning, and if you do happen to win, they will give you a complimentary room, a Trojan horse, disguised to take some of their money back during your stay.

These techniques are designed to distract from reality and keep you engaged for someone else's purpose. Pinocchio to Geppetto—Cut the strings. Learn to put your phone down or say, "Not right now." Disconnect and remain disconnected. We are in the age of social media push notifications, ringtones, dating apps, and video streaming services. It is necessary to move from one task to another to achieve balance. Still, when it is time to focus, you must be able to identify and eliminate all distractions.

There is a reason distractions threaten your work output. It takes a significant amount of time to regain focus after being sidetracked. In the previous chapter, we emphasized the necessity of capitalizing on your motivation by maximizing your level of discipline. Now allow me to illustrate why you must avoid going in five directions simultaneously.

Concentration is quieting the noise to sharpen your vision and enhance mental clarity. Imagine shooting a free throw: it's a free, uncontested shot. You don't have to rush; your shot won't be blocked. You could practice the shot a billion times until you couldn't miss it if you tried, but worrying about the crowd, your shoes, breathing, the temperature, your significant other, and the play that sent you to the line are all factors that could make you susceptible to messing up something simple.

Relax, Focus, and Concentrate

Establish a routine, but make sure it challenges you just enough to keep you hungry, motivated, engaged, and undeterred. Maintain your rigid flexibility. I repeat, maintain your rigid flexibility.

There is a reason you decided to set your sights on whatever goal and path you chose. Remaining cognizant of those goals will help you stay focused and grind it out. Remember why you started. Think about it. Was it money? A better career? More time with family? Personal achievement? More flexibility? Or maybe it was becoming legendary and making history.

"You become what you believe."
—Oprah Winfrey[13]

The Power of Believing

I became a proponent of affirmations and manifestations once I became aware and began to embrace the psychological impact of implementing these practices. The mind is so powerful that you give life to the things you focus on; that is the power of believing. We were made in the image of The Creator and have the power to create.

Affirmation (practicing self-empowerment through positive thinking in the present tense with specific and personal ideas) aligns and focuses your

---

[13] Oprah Winfrey, "You Become What You Believe. You Are Where You Are Today in Your Life Based on Everything You Have Believed," QuoteFancy, accessed September 23, 2023, https://quotefancy.com/quote/879511/Oprah-Winfrey-You-become-what-you-believe-You-are-where-you-are-today-in-your-life-based.

thoughts. Manifestation is the act of believing in a manner so powerful that your predominant thoughts become tangible in the physical world. You can maximize your ability by controlling what you concentrate on with absolute focus and belief.

Don't be a soft target, susceptible to random distracting conversations and influence. Through advanced tactics of malignant psychology, advertisers and other influencers can covertly display flash messages, use celebrity endorsements, alter your attention span, and pass their ideas as your own. So, take a minute to sort out and clearly define *your* intentions and proceed without anyone else's influential recommendations. Then remember that regardless of everything, the things you don't focus on don't exist. By the same token, the opposite is true. That which you give attention, you also give life. Now that you have the necessary focus and concentration, it is time to bring your thoughts and ideas to fruition.

I loved every aspect of being in the US Air Force; distinguished career, freedom, complete autonomy to learn, travel, meet new people (or not), experience other cultures, and learn foreign languages. I was in my early twenties, and it felt like a dream come true. I had structure, room to grow while learning from mistakes (that's part of living), and an exciting time and unforgettable experiences everywhere I was stationed while supporting an elite, lethal organization. This is what pride feels like.

I have a few remarkable stories about my dealings with the other branches (especially the Army), but for now, let's consider my experience with my Marine Corps brothers. While stationed in Okinawa, Japan, I met military personnel from all branches of service. One of my closest friends was John Kennedy, whom I still view as my extremely talented, bad-ass little brother. Another friend was Donte Smith, a US Marine. I learned a great deal about the marine brotherhood while drinking and partying. I would fight every weekend (with marines against other marines and anybody else who wanted some action), but the guys I fought against would never come looking for me. There was never any animosity, at least to my knowledge. Whatever happened from week to week was not carried forward with hostile intentions. This helped me develop a thicker skin and a more powerful mindset when dealing with life.

> **Key Takeaway:** Be tough, and don't sweat the small stuff.

Many Veterans with whom I've had discourse didn't like their time serving; however, I don't share the same sentiments of regret and confinement. Prior to enlisting, we thought we knew what the experience would be like, but we had yet to learn. Regardless, we were willing to sacrifice for the benefit of our country. It was the best decision we could make to improve our lives for the better as we saw the future, and it gave us a feeling of purpose. But in retrospect, the experience was different than we thought it would be, at least for me. It was a different world. I asked many questions, but I had no idea how the experience would change me. The discipline portion was a given, but there were numerous unknown aspects with tremendous benefit that I'm grateful for.

NFL (Not for Long)

When I read or hear stories, I typically only hear about the author's or narrator's successes, but I will tell you about one of my failures. It's okay; I can take it. Thanks in advance for your condolences because the following dream died.

I left the military to pursue my dream as a pro football player but did not dedicate enough time, energy, or resources to achieving this goal. I worked out often and did a lot of groundwork with a friend of mine named Torrance Heggie (I call him T). His wife was a marine stationed at Quantico. At the time, I supported Marine Corps Systems Command (MARCORSYSCOM) Battle Space Management operations, which was how we met. Our schedules lined up. I would train when I got off work. First, I would hit the weights before heading outside for some groundwork.

There was an NFL Combine in Pittsburgh, Pennsylvania, and I decided I was ready for a tryout. My idea was to use that as a springboard to gain experience and get my foot in the door for the NFL. I was ambitious and strong, and nothing was stopping me from going. My older sister accompanied me on the trip. We had a great ride up, but the rest of the journey was like a nightmare. I didn't sleep well, but that didn't bother me much. We arrived right on time, which was a mistake. The event started as soon as we got there. I didn't plan, warm up, or survey the area, which later proved to be a tremendous oversight that contributed to the setback. I could have just called it a wash, sat idly in the background as a bystander, and used that knowledge I gained to return more prepared and ready.

But what happened? We began the event with a short thirty-second warm-up lap and followed it up by running the forty-yard dash for time. The first time I ran, I was as fast as lightning, and after I ran, the coaches looked at each other like, *damn, he's fast*. I couldn't wait for the second run. I was cold on the first one, so I figured I would only do better the second time if I had two or three minutes to rest, but the brief period is like a blurred memory. It is as if I immediately ran again, even though I had to wait in line for my turn.

All I remember is starting strong. I didn't stand up too quickly; I stayed low and kept my feet moving while looking forward. Then suddenly, I heard a pop—or more like *felt* it. I pulled my groin, and it hurt like hell. It felt like I ripped part of my leg off, but I kept practicing to stave off the thought that my dream of making it pro was instantly over. The NFL is a fast-paced environment. *"It's a little different from college, huh John Boy?"* At least, that is what I told myself.

I mismanaged the ensuing events of my injury. I started focusing on other things to make the recent failure less painful to deal with instead of handling it as I would now; concentrating all of my focus, time, and energy into figuring out what went wrong, accepting responsibility for my tremendous oversight, producing a solid plan, and committing to the process.

I had the discipline to establish and follow a routine, but there were several things that I was missing. For instance, I didn't seek advice from a healthcare professional to train more effectively, enhance my performance, and assist in my recovery. I knew several people I could have sought guidance from to determine the necessary steps to recuperate or my chances (if any) of ever playing again, but I decided to let my ego guide me. I knew I would make it to the league because I was insanely quick, strong as an ox, and determined to let nothing stand in my way. But I failed, and this dream never came to fruition. Just because you are committed to your chosen path doesn't mean it will lead you to a desirable destination.

> **Key Takeaway:** Wise men seek wise counsel.

What's your trajectory? You don't need differential calculus to determine if you're on track. The question I posed was regarding your current course or focused path, on which there can be several variables and influences to consider. Be wise and put your ego aside (for now) and do whatever it takes to be certain that what you expect and work towards will be the result provided. You must follow processes to accurately plan, prepare, and evaluate. Be smart. Know your data and numbers. You can't say, "I just know," because that is a naive perspective and will only lead to epic and catastrophic failure.

Constant Effort

Let's wrap it up, but I need to ask a favor of you before we do. Start now, take it slow, and make immediate changes. Don't concern yourself with what you need to do for the rest of your life. Just live in the moment and enjoy getting stronger and mentally tougher by pushing yourself. One thing that I remind myself of daily is to apply "Constant Effort". This is something that I mentioned a few times throughout the chapters because it is one of the things that keeps my fire burning. This concept is so significant that I could have named the entire book after these two words: "Constant Effort".

You don't need to move a million miles an hour or make provisions to do everything simultaneously. In fact, the faster you move, the more you will miss. Just take it slow, push yourself, and keep putting in the work, and you will be amazed at what you accomplish over time.

Are you ready to get serious about your life while maximizing your discipline and concentration? You have a fantastic idea that will change the world; all you need is a little more time, right? Well—Today's your lucky day, and I'm going to show you how to take some of your time back. Are you listening? Good, because this is going to sound familiar. A few minutes a day will make a tremendous impact over time, but before you get started, you must pick an area to completely devote all your attention; at least for a few minutes. Listen, I know what I'm talking about. This is how I mastered the stock market. Trust me. Name one thing that you want to do and fully commit to it.

I am talking about a few minutes a day. Whether you are stuck in traffic, watching TV, on your lunch break, setting your morning alarm thirty minutes ahead of schedule, or arriving at work a few minutes early, you have the time, but you must decide to commit. That's the first step. Give yourself some of your conscious thought, energy, and effort. Don't spend all your time, more than half of life's waking moments, fulfilling somebody else's purpose and dreams; that makes you dependent because you have identified and resonated with insignificant areas of comfort. Spoiler alert! You don't have as much time as you think. Focus now and get to work!

Wake-up. Kill Sh*t. Repeat.

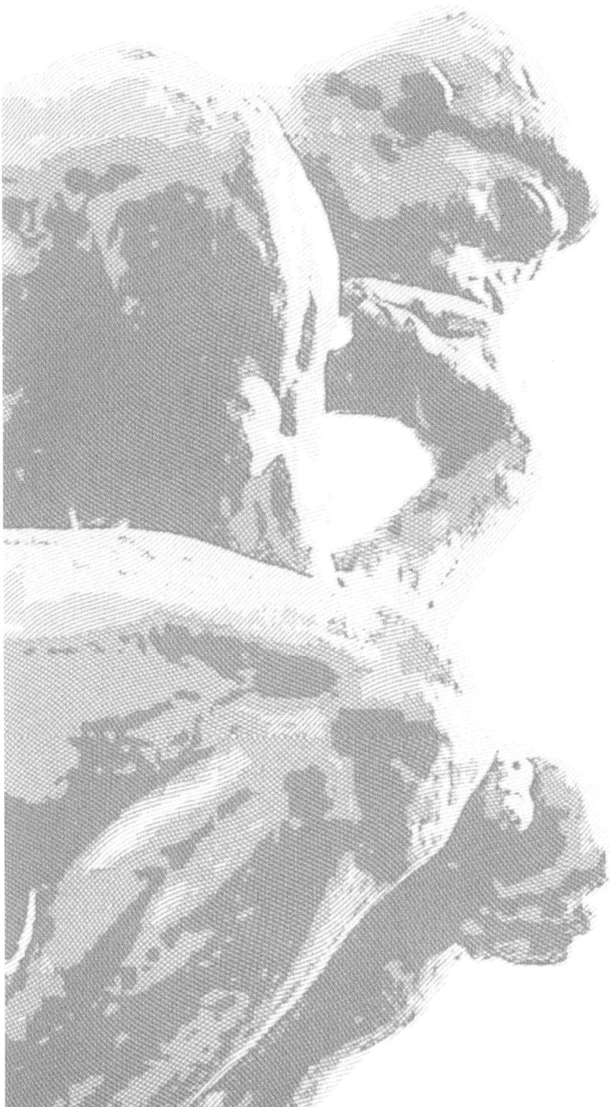

Chapter 4

WORK ETHIC

> "Outwork your self-doubt."
>
> —Alex Hormozi[14]

HOW SHOULD YOU RESPOND WHEN FACED WITH SETBACKS AND OBSTACLES?

What do you want more than anything in this world? What is your big dream? What is that seemingly indomitable task you have been unable to start, let alone finish? If you knew you could not fail, what would you be willing to do to make that happen?

Can you do more, and how much pain can you take?

I asked if you could do more and how much pain you could take because I've observed people quit prematurely after performing a myriad of activities. They believed they were tired but then felt a sudden burst of energy upon realizing that an emergency or another unforeseeable occurrence required immediate attention. What I grew to understand is that they weren't tired at all. They were tired of exerting energy in a

---

[14] Hormozi, Alex, "You Don't Become Confident by Shouting Affirmations in the Mirror, but by Having a Stack of Undeniable Proof That You Are Who You Say You Are. Outwork Your Self Doubt," Twitter, October 29, 2022, 12:34 pm, accessed September 23, 2023, https://twitter.com/AlexHormozi/status/1586441477952921600.

particular area, but they had much more effort to give. If you routinely stop when a challenge becomes painful or difficult, you will never grow from it. But you'll get stronger if you take the pain and hold the weight a little longer. I say push yourself in every area.

> **Key Takeaway:** The long-term benefits and results of consistent, focused effort will shock you.

Let me be more specific. *Weakness is a state of mind; strength is a measure of your capability, albeit unlimited.* Most people succumb to temptation (a sign of weakness) because the subconscious mind is programmable. If you repeatedly quit, it will become second nature and habitual. Similarly, at first sight of a tempting, comfortable, familiar, or shiny new thing, you will respond in a manner that does not reflect your true strength or full potential.

Do not seek comfort. Instead, choose strength and willpower over fragility. Most people fall victim to temptation because the subconscious mind is programmable and formed out of habit.

From my experience, individuals who try to break unwanted habits, like nicotine addiction or alcoholism, revert to those old ways when they encounter a moderate degree of pain or stress. When people regress to old habits at the first sign of difficulty, I tell them they would experience that difficulty anyway, so their excuses are empty and inadequate. You will suffer atrocities, lose those you thought you couldn't live without, experience road rage, find yourself stuck in traffic, face insurmountable odds, or experience something that will piss you off (if you choose to allow it to do so). Whatever the case, the list is infinite. But guess what? So is your capability.

Tip: Practicing delayed gratification increases willpower.

> "If you don't have time to do it right,
> you must have time to do it over."
>
> —John Wooden[15]

If you complete a task, why not give 100 percent effort if you will accomplish the same activity regardless? Think about it. Concentrating will minimize the possibility of errors and rework. Devoting focused attention will also decrease the time and energy you exert on that task if you embrace it and give it your undivided attention. Contrary to your belief, you are not preserving energy by doing something and only giving half the effort. Adjust, start performing at your highest level, and watch your neural pathways become automatically rewired to execute with maximum efficiency.

#NODAYSOFFPAYSOFF

When I was around six years old, in southeast Washington, DC, I saw the older kids make money by passing out advertisements for the local grocery store. They were the happiest kids and the first to the ice cream truck. I started invading their territory to pass out flyers in the early afternoon before they could do so.

I thought they would confront me out of anger and decided to proceed irrespective of the consequences, but they didn't seem to care. I was much younger than they were but still grinding. I didn't have much choice. Put yourself in my shoes. As an adult, imagine going to sleep, knowing that when you awaken, the refrigerator will still be empty, and you will go hungry. Now, imagine facing the same challenge as a kid. I would sometimes make enough money to feed my brother and sisters,

---

[15] John Wooden, "If You Don't Have Time to Do It Right, When Will You Have Time to Do It over?," BrainyQuote, accessed September 23, 2023, https://www.brainyquote.com/quotes/john_wooden_384653.

not every day, but occasionally. Soon, I realized I did not have to be hungry and wait for somebody to feed us. All it took was a little work.

I began to notice the numerous methods people used to generate capital. By the sixth grade, I was already well into the third year of my fourth hustle—selling newspapers in Southern Pines, North Carolina. This was referred to as "bussin' *Pilots*." The *Pilot* was the local newspaper's name and 'bussin' referred to busting your hump to make a sale.

I noticed that to sell the newspaper, I would have to pay fifteen cents to make twenty-five cents, and I realized I had to buy the newspapers to sell them again. It was not easy, but I was very charismatic, even at an early age, so my people skills helped me excel in that business.

Otis Cagle and his brother Greg also sold newspapers. But for them, it was more of a delivery subscription service, and they would disappear and make a lot of money in a brief period. This perplexed me. I didn't initially understand why. Consistency is vital. They had customers who expected their newspaper early, and they always ran their routes. There was no getting in. I tried several times, and those customers would let me know, "Otis beat you to it." Even at my first stop, they would say "no thanks" because it was not about them getting the paper anymore; it was their loyalty to their dependable delivery personnel.

I recall one occasion when I sold to one of their regular customers and got about five dollars for one newspaper. I remember Otis showing up as soon as I completed the transaction, and I laughed and said, "I beat you!" He went in and came back out in seconds, smiling with a handful of dollars. I was confused. He didn't say anything; he just resumed his route.

Key Takeaway: Consistency builds trust over time—everybody's watching.

> "If you really look closely, most overnight successes took a long time."
>
> —Steve Jobs[16]

Everything that takes time requires patience. As a young adult, I wasted a substantial amount of time and money by taking an extended break to clear my head while making several impulsive decisions. My only focus was having fun and doing what I wanted. I remember going to the bank and withdrawing a few thousand dollars every few days, and this didn't include what I was spending on my debit card. I remember Penny, the bank teller, looking at me with concern as my account slowly diminished. She recommended a financial advisor, but I received no financial advice other than another account setup recommendation.

When Dawn, the branch manager, and Penny asked again if I needed assistance, I replied, "I got this," but I did not have it. I was spiraling out of control. I didn't have a plan, and any money I made previously or during that time was touch and go. If you have never had money, you cannot relate. You do what you want when you want and how you want. Freedom.

Admitting my spiral, I slowed down as much as possible and decided to produce a definitive financial plan, which worked better than expected. It didn't take long before I gained solid footing. I soon accumulated more money than ever because I also spent less, which is a terrific way to put yourself in a better position and improve your circumstances, enhance your lifestyle, and save. Money is a tool. It has a purpose. Use it wisely. The goal is not to make more money just for the sake of having more to spend, right? That type of thinking is adolescent. Motivation, discipline, and a focused dynamic plan will keep everything balanced. Still, it is challenging without

---

[16] Abdallah Alaili, "If You Really Look Closely, Most Overnight Successes Took a Long Time. – Steve Jobs," Entrepreneur Post, November 11, 2020, https://www.entrepreneurpost.com/2020/11/11/if-you-really-look-closely-most-overnight-successes-took-a-long-time-steve-jobs/; Petter Loken, "Lessons from Steve Jobs," January 6, 2021, accessed September 23, 2023, https://www.petterloken.no/post/lessons-from-steve-jobs.

patience, which is necessary to see the fruits of your labor and keep you maintaining or growing.

If you don't know what you want to do, or you know but don't have a plan, that's okay, but get one ASAP! Plans go on paper. Remember that. Talk is cheap. Anybody can talk. It gets you nowhere and means nothing. Ultimately, you'll have nothing to show for it without discipline, focus, and a remarkable work ethic. Like a skilled tactician, your vision will require a solid yet flexible strategy; *a series of intertwined tactics that evolve with intricate detail and meticulous calculation.* Without a solid plan and consistent effort, any idea formed is one based solely on theory and perception.

Regardless, the grind must be the integral constant. Unrelenting persistence is the key to inexorability. *How you are in one thing, you are in all things. Start* slow, but start now, and don't let up. I will say that again because this has become my mantra. Ask yourself now, *what is holding me back?* Why have you not at least put pen to paper? Why wait?

Start building your plan and strategizing immediately. The only reason for any hesitation is taking the time necessary to determine the best strategy based on your anticipated result. But even then, there's no reason to wait. If you are continually thinking of your idea and delaying putting it on paper while it's only in your head—you are still waiting. I am warning you: start now, or you'll regret it. You can thank me later.

Limitless

Again, there are 86,400 seconds in a day; pick one and own it and every moment that is to follow. Focus on your vision, select the best method of execution based on your skills and resources, and get it done. Listen, I can see your future, and I'm telling you that you can accomplish anything if you are willing to focus, work, and persevere. If you are serious about achieving something, shouldn't you want it bad enough to do more than just talk about it?

When you apply your highest level of effort, it will fuel your focus. Some of you think that what you are is what you will be. Don't limit your potential by confining yourself to a world created within an imaginative reality of limitations. Those walls do not exist. Don't put a physical limitation on your mental capability. Your mind will believe whatever you tell it. Feed your thoughts accordingly.

You will adapt to doing less or get accustomed to doing more. Why not get used to doing more? As mentioned in Chapter One, *effort determines performance*. I don't want a break and don't look forward to slowing down. My mind never stops. I'm always working and constantly adapting to what I need to do and the most efficient way to get it done. With that said, there's one aspect that never changes: My willingness. I'm always ready to do whatever it takes. I have learned how to focus and push through anything. Every morning, I wake up driven with my finger on the trigger.

But how did I get like this? Maybe it was one of my prior brushes with death. Was it falling out of the window? I don't know. What I am sure of, though, is that anybody can be motivated. Motive, from the Latin word *motivus*, means "the thing that causes you to act." What is your driving force? If what you're doing is important, it will get done no matter what, and if it isn't, it will be evident and reflected in your progress. You aren't promised tomorrow. Time is running out, and if that thought doesn't motivate you to stop procrastinating, nothing will.

Quick Question: What's the difference between somebody who has transitioned to the next life and somebody doing nothing while they are here? Let's shift our focus to you. What are you doing? Maybe you don't take your life seriously. Think about it. If you never set goals or do so passively but aren't actively striving to achieve them, you don't take your life seriously. So again, what are you doing? Answer the next question before continuing.

What is your Five-Year Plan?

Is it written somewhere, on a thumb drive, saved on a computer, on your phone, in an email you sent yourself, or just in your head? If it's only in your head, that is lazy. If you don't know your purpose, that's not a good enough excuse for inaction. There are plenty of people to help, good energy to spread, products to sell, ideas to turn into products, whatever you like, are good at, or constantly talk about.

Yeah, I am talking to you. You, reading this. You told several people that you are thinking about starting this business doing this new cool or purposeful thing, but what are you waiting for? Or you do not know how to do 'XYZ.' That is an empty excuse. You can use your phone to access the internet. Do some research. I am calling you out.

You can't expect somebody to read for you. And if you aren't doing the bare minimum research to get started, what makes you think you have what it takes to be successful? Your journey will require your determination at some point. Remaining conscious of your 'why' will keep your thoughts purposeful and your actions relentless.

Regain Control

If you made it this far in the reading, you have what it takes to make meaningful changes in your life. It doesn't matter what anyone told you that may have destroyed your self-esteem or what experiences contributed to your limiting beliefs. *Self-deception is a mirror without reflection.* Quit reminding yourself of your pain to justify your inaction or lack of motivation. Get that crap out of your head. Nothing is holding you back other than—you. None of your ideas require capital to get started. They require focus.

Plans go on paper. Business plans are free. Do you have a great business idea? Do you have a business plan? Why not? Maybe you aren't as devoted as you thought. Creating a to-do list requires nothing more than diligence and consistency. It is effortless to place a phone call and ask questions. There are countless free information resources. Research the top five ways to accomplish anything, and you will generate millions of results. So, what is the problem? I'm referring to one aspect of your life—your work ethic. Take small, affordable steps, but be serious about your goals. Stop talking and *shhh…show me*. Better yet, show yourself. Talk less and do more. Let your actions speak.

> "Those who are successful overcome
> their fears and take action!"
>
> —Jay-Z[17]

That feeling of fear is all in your mind. Don't believe me? Try this. Do whatever you are afraid of doing, and if what you fear will happen occurs, feel free to quit and revert to doing nothing. But if I'm right, I want you to decide to commit time and focused energy to pursue your goals. Taking action by testing the waters prohibits you from hiding behind excuses and living in a comfort zone. Read that again.

ADAPTING

I am sure you noticed, but in case you missed it, everything we have covered so far is to prepare you mentally for what is to come. By now, you are likely motivated to act while striking with pinpoint accuracy, and you will continue to push forward and persevere until you obtain your intended results.

> "We are what we repeatedly do.
> Excellence, then, is not an act but a habit."
>
> —Will Durant[18]

---

[17] Ryan Austin, "Top 10 Jay-Z Quotes About Success," *Deeper Freedom* (blog), accessed September 23, 2023, https://deeperfreedom.com/jay-z-quotes-about-success/.

[18] Sophia Merton, ""We Are What We Repeatedly Do" - Meaning and History - Stoic Quotes," StoicQuotes.com, February 28, 2023, https://stoicquotes.com/we-are-what-we-repeatedly-do/.

My younger sister, Imani, calls me 'Mr. Figure it Out.' I have supreme confidence in my abilities. As I previously mentioned, I enjoy the problem-solving process. Some issues are more difficult to decipher than others; however, these minor challenges only require a little strategic thinking to produce a solution.

The following line will be disruptive, but the words to follow are certain to restore order. *You may never receive the results you want, regardless of how focused you are or how hard you work.* That is until you produce and follow the right strategy. If your first approach doesn't work, who cares?

Take your time, concentrate, and step back if you don't see desirable results. Be observant, consider what areas need improvement, and brainstorm additional methods to accomplish your goals. If you can't go under, go over, go around, or go through. Just don't stop; there is always a way. Your job is to figure it out.

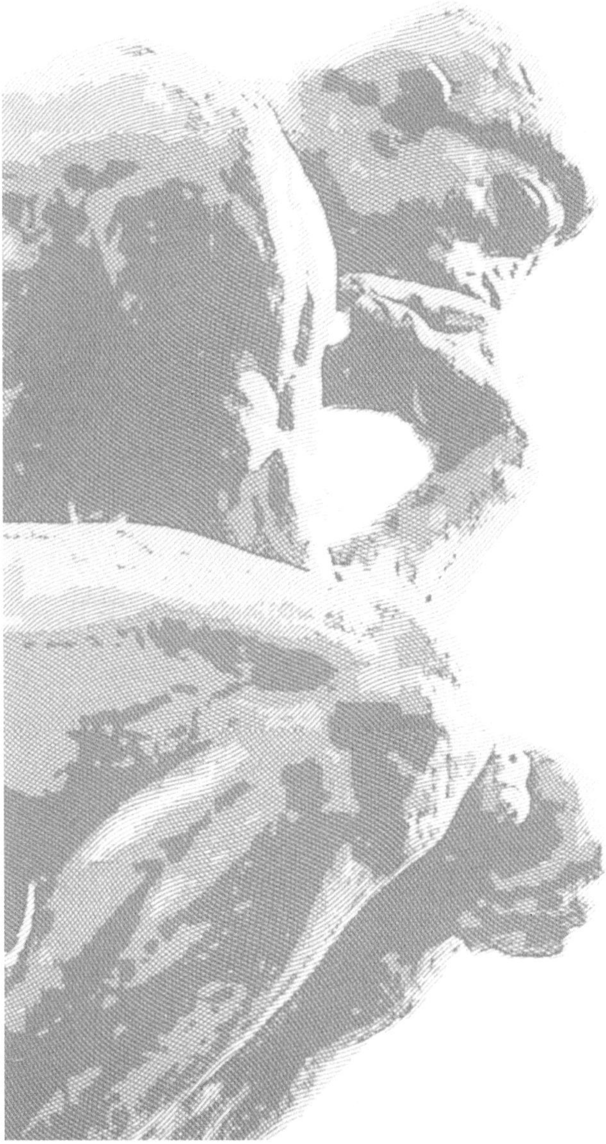

Chapter 5

Strategy and Positioning

> "It is not the strongest that survives; but the species that is able best to adapt and adjust."
>
> —Leon C. Megginson[19]

What is Strategy?

A strategy is a general action plan designed to achieve one or more specific goals. These actions help guide the decision-making process for task prioritization and resource selection. A strategy also helps ensure maximum efficiency when combining different resources or skills to support an objective.

How do you leverage your available resources to benefit your strategic advantage? That question may seem like a lot to grasp, but it's simple. If you're like me, you have primarily heard the word *strategy* discussed during movie scenes involving elaborate military operations. You may assume since you are no commanding officer that this level of analytical complexity is way out of your scope. Right? Wrong! You are a lot better at strategizing than you think.

---

[19] Leon C. Megginson, "Lessons from Europe for American Business," *The Southwestern Social Science Quarterly* 44, no. 1 (1963): 4, http://www.jstor.org/stable/42866937.

If you have ever run errands, you have had to think strategically. You probably wrote out a quick list before starting your journey, going to the locations farther away from your final stop and working toward your destination. This allowed you to save gas and time. If you had a lot of running around to do and had to purchase groceries, you probably saved grocery shopping for last because you had perishable items. But before you went grocery shopping, you met up with a friend for lunch at a location you selected that was close to your last stop. Smart thinking. However, this was not only smart thinking, but also thinking strategically. Well done. You are officially ready for war. Let's talk more about my experience with strategy.

While deployed, a former team member, Cory Rogers, reminded me how chess pieces moved on a chessboard (my dad went over this once when I was young), and I couldn't get enough of the game. It was like the board game version of *Call of Duty*. Now, let's talk strategy. I was stationed at Tallil Air Base, located off the Main Supply Route, just north of the Iraqi prison Camp Bucca. I was the only electronic warfare specialist (pawn) supporting the southern region after Dobby Gaiski, the previous site lead, gave me a light review of everything I needed to know and left a few weeks too early.

I worked in excess of twelve hours a day and didn't mind. It wasn't as if I could somehow see my family or head to the beach when I got off. I was at war, and my mind adjusted. I wanted to ensure that the frontline soldiers (other pawns) were protected and that I had the knowledge and access to the extensive resources and support required to perform my mission. Ground forces were experiencing more frequent attacks due to the emerging threat of IEDs, incoming artillery shells, and rockets. In response, headquarters, Camp Balad, sent much-needed reinforcements (power pieces).

Once I saw that these men needed little to no instruction, I moved from "Johnny Warlock," the only ground system expert, to the manager of civilian personnel (power piece). This was all part of a small component of the dynamic big picture. My role was vital yet small in the larger scheme of things. This was strategy. I realized why teamwork was essential and how individual wants and needs, however important, paled in comparison to the omniscient perspective.

Rigid Flexibility

Remember to determine your ultimate objective, then plan your attack after you analyze and align your perceived strengths and resources accordingly. Your plan can be altered, but the primary goal should be close to what it was initially. Spend more time with the vision of where you want to be, and you will navigate like a star running back outmaneuvering opponents to meet his primary objective: more yards gained, inch by inch. He may try to score on every play, but he watches the short-term goals: the immediate obstacles. Note that his overall plan hasn't changed; however, he makes minor necessary adjustments while remaining focused on the initial goal.

They say life is a gamble, but why gamble when you can control the odds and determine the outcome? Some people live with one thing in mind: pushing themselves, devoting their time and attention, ignoring temptation, evading comfort, remaining focused, planning, executing, and adjusting while moving forward and finding balance. There is nothing better than having a solid plan in place. You can adjust on the fly to adapt to changing circumstances. Embrace changes. Think realistically, design and modify your road map's true heading to take you where you want to go. Your dynamic strategy helps ensure your plans and goals align. In life, things happen, and plans should change accordingly. Adapt and learn to adjust.

Do you have questions or comments about any part of what you have read? I invite readers of this book to comment. Just scan the QR code on this book's rear cover, click on *contact info*, message me, and I will respond.

Wait, was that a social media growth strategy that I just implemented? You tell me. Did I provide a way to accomplish one or more of my objectives by providing a call to action while attempting to insert a thought inside of your subconscious mind (through repetition and association) while simultaneously offering a helpful way to engage with you to provide clarity? Do you think so? Well, I guess it was. However, a strategy doesn't have to be a mechanism to kill two or more birds with one stone. It could be as straightforward as prohibiting yourself from eating at restaurants so you can meal prep and save money. This will also allow you to spend less while enjoying the foods you want.

Over three years ago, I deleted my social media accounts. My purpose was to focus more. Simple, right? It only required a small amount of discipline. But guess what? It has proven to be one of my most productive decisions. No, I don't suggest deleting all your accounts and going into *full ninja mode* like I did unless you feel other areas of your life deserve more attention.

"If you're going through hell, keep going!"
—Winston Churchill[20]

Take a look at your current situation. Remember that lost loved one, that breakup, that period of depression? Remember your lowest low? Don't revisit it, but we all have a point that was our most memorable and emotionally devastating. But as time passes, emotions decrease, pain subsides, perspectives change, and we live, learn, and grow in unimaginable ways. Look at your life at this very moment. Did you ever think you would be where you are now or make it through that stuff? No. Of course not. Especially not at that time, but you didn't give up.

JUST KEEP GOING

I am a huge proponent and advocate of suicide awareness and prevention. We can take many routes, but there is only one best way. No matter how you view a situation, you may produce several viable options. However—there is only <u>one</u> best way, and giving up is not it. I don't believe in permanent solutions to temporary problems. I have overcome some

---

[20] Geoff Loftus, "If You're Going Through Hell, Keep Going - Winston Churchill," Forbes, May 9, 2012, https://www.forbes.com/sites/geoffloftus/2012/05/09/if-youre-going-through-hell-keep-going-winston-churchill/?sh=29db1498d549.

exceedingly challenging times. Guess what? I kept swinging. All I know is that I'm never giving up. Be patient and keep fighting!

Let's consider all that and decide, based on the obstacles you have faced and overcome and the confidence you feel when you reflect on those previous instances, that you are not stopping and will continue to fight, no matter what!

What is your Driving Force?

I've had a few brushes with death, and I am not scared to die—but I am thankful for every breath. Decide what you want and go after it. Do what you love and be around those who support and encourage you. Or better yet, know your worth and encourage and push yourself. Time is limited, so don't waste it by procrastinating. When you get the courage to chase your dreams, start that business, move to a new city, or change careers, go for it! You have the plan; plan the work and work the plan. And when you do, what's next? You guessed it! Time to execute.

Ready, Aim, Fire!

We have spent more than enough time getting our minds right. We are now ready to walk through walls. If our focus gets any sharper, we will be able to see the future. We are motivated, disciplined, focused, and prepared to give constant effort while considering strategies and tactics to help us navigate and rip through obstacles. You are ready, and it's time for some action!

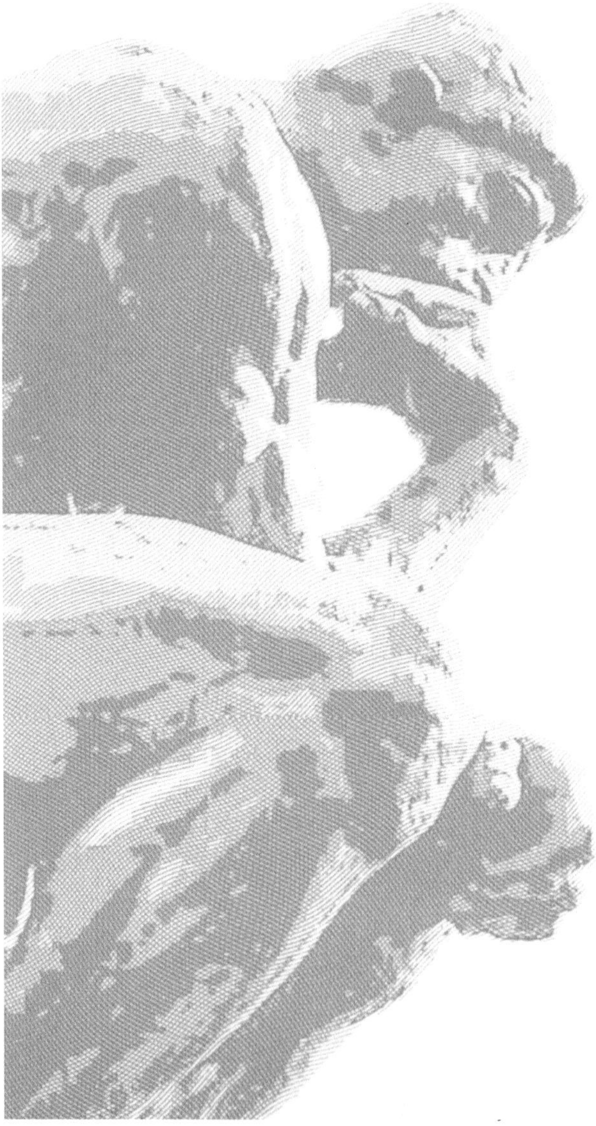

Chapter 6

EXECUTION

"You may delay, but time will not."
—Benjamin Franklin[21]

WHY IS THE ABILITY TO TAKE ACTION AND MAKE THINGS HAPPEN ESSENTIAL?

What do you want more than anything? Are you working on that? If the answer is no, then why not? If so, then keep it up. That's a hell of a conversation starter.

Most people will look in amazement when asked what they want more than anything. It is logical to assume that you would not be doing anything else, especially if you knew it was possible to live out your dreams. Don't let fear of failure, aversion to change, priorities, lack of confidence, inopportune timing, or social expectations stand in your way.

About fear of failure: everybody fails at something. How quickly can you learn and recover to move forward? That's the real question. Most dreams take two things: brains and determination. We forge our dreams in the fire of our willpower. The majority spend so much time overthinking that work never gets done because they take themselves out of action and

---

[21] Benjamin Franklin, "You May Delay, but Time Will Not," BrainyQuote, accessed September 23, 2023, https://www.brainyquote.com/quotes/benjamin_franklin_101831.

self-sabotage by concentrating on what could go wrong instead of what may go right.

Negative thinking and overanalyzing are counterproductive. Analyzing is beneficial; it helps you fine-tune your strategy while your moves are imminent. However, overanalyzing is excessive and often results in procrastination or miscalculation, which is your way of either prolonging inaction or not facing your fear.

"You miss 100 percent of the shots you don't take."
—Wayne Gretzky[22]

Some of the best ideas I have ever heard were forgotten, dwindled, or died because the creators failed to act. Don't share your precious visions with anyone. I am sure those in your inner circle have your best interests at heart and want to see you succeed, but envy and jealousy are Siamese twins. Also, if you are so motivated that you must tell someone, you should refocus that energy into action. Instead of talking, try this:

"The young do not know enough to be prudent, and therefore they attempt the impossible—and achieve it, generation after generation."
—Pearl S. Buck[23]

---

[22] Paul B. Brown, "'You Miss 100% of the Shots You Don't Take.' You Need to Start Shooting at Your Goals," Forbes, January 12, 2014., https://www.forbes.com/sites/actiontrumpseverything/2014/01/12/you-miss-100-of-the-shots-you-dont-take-so-start-shooting-at-your-goal/?sh=26629b116a40.

[23] Pearl S. Buck, "The Young Do Not Know Enough to Be Prudent, and Therefore They Attempt the Impossible - and Achieve It, Generation After Generation," BrainyQuote, accessed September 23, 2023, https://www.brainyquote.com/quotes/pearl_s_buck_161681.

30-DAY FOCUS CHALLENGE

DAY 1: GOAL SELECTION

1. Decide on a goal. It doesn't matter if you're indecisive; indecision is an immature response and requires no growth or acceptance of responsibility. If you have kids, they will mimic your behavior. They hear your words but learn the most from your actions or demonstrated knowledge. If you have five things that you are selecting from, pick one. I was in your exact position, facing an identical dilemma before authoring this book. Despite having a list of hundreds of goals, dreams, and ideas, I picked this one. Make a decision. You don't have as much time as you think. Those windows of opportunity are constantly closing.

DAY 2: THE MASTERPLAN

2. Develop a plan. Start by brainstorming words and thoughts on paper. Write down everything it takes to achieve your chosen goal, enabling you to visualize all your options. Next, arrange your list categorically, then put it on a completion timeline and stick to it.

DAY 3-29: MONITOR AND TRACK

3. Use a to-do list to track and cross-reference each task with your completion timeline based on the following action required and suspense date.
4. Monitor your progress and mark items as complete as you go.
5. In the process, keep your environment clean, clear, and organized, reducing anxiety and helping you calm your mind and focus your thoughts.

Day 30: Increase your Confidence

6. Look at your progress. Remember where you started and reflect upon how far you have advanced. At this point, you have established a fundamental routine and developed an extremely healthy habit. Be proud of yourself, decide on another goal (and start date), and remember to celebrate your accomplishments.

I do whatever I can to enable me to take immediate action. I will conduct extensive internet research to learn how to do something or acquire a new skill. If I can't find it there, I will search video-sharing services and forums. There is always a way. Figure it out. Kill all excuses, stay focused, and take action. Of course, distractions are inevitable, but you are supposed to see challenges as moments to gain experience. Problems provide growth opportunities. Taking action is not just looking at everything positively because some things are catastrophic, but there is always a beneficial takeaway. Your mission is to find it and use it to your advantage.

Blinding Ambition

I enjoy what I do, but I work my ass off. My ambition is blinding. I'm not open to unsolicited advice or recommendations from those who have never done it and hypocritically teach theory. For example, I don't know any business professors with successful businesses). If I don't ask, don't offer. Hopefully, you just learned something about me, not as a keepsake but as a commonality for ending conversations early, taking space, keeping your distance, and getting more serious about making progress and handling your business.

Somewhere between trying to figure my life out and wanting to do more to help people reinforce their minds, I began to read energy primarily from being observant. I can tell if someone is serious about achieving their goals, motivated, just talking, putting on a show, ambitious, focused, cunning, or in need of encouragement. Sadly, you can't help everyone. Comfort is the currency for the slothful, and many are comfortable with nothing; but it's sad when people live without a dream. Without a plan to achieve a set objective, what could you do but aimlessly wander? I would hate that feeling of walking in circles. Busy people don't get the most done—productive people do.

Becoming a motivational speaker was not something I planned for. It began with social media. I would randomly post entertaining and motivational content, but everything I emitted reflected my perspective. I liked helping people but didn't like wasting time, so I decided that the content needed to be a combination of impactful and uplifting. Even if it was just a one-liner, that's time out of my life and an opportunity to make a difference. I recognized the power of belief, encouragement, focus, deliberate intent, and consistent effort.

My brother-in-law Billy Boots is a fighter like no other. He just beat cancer and calls me '*The Motivation Champ.*' I talked to him while he was undergoing radiation treatment, but I wasn't just trying to lift his spirits; I was reminding him of what I saw as characteristics in his behavior and thinking pattern. We all need a reminder of who we are to sharpen our focus. And when fighting anything, remember the world is watching. When we are kicking ass, we may inspire others to do the same.

TIME TO GET SERIOUS

A few years ago, when I initially began drafting this book, I thought it was the best idea in the world. After picking the title (which has changed three times), I couldn't wait to finish it. I told a few people about it and figured I could get it done whenever I could fit it into my schedule. I thought I was serious, but how could I have been if it did not matter when it got done? I could've worked on it forever and almost did. What was taking so long? I didn't commit to the process. I needed a writing timeline, a solid schedule, and a completion date. With that said, I had a solid outline and some encouraging notes and takeaways from my life, but it was far from a book. When I realized this, I quickly adjusted. I started working on it daily, stuck to my strategic initiative, and, voilà—I got it done.

Start small but start now. This book is not intended to be a panacea for the unmotivated but an accurate account of what has helped me decide to keep swinging against all odds. And I'm not stopping, no matter what. Have you ever heard the saying, "*You are one decision away from a totally different life?*" Imagine scheduling your priorities; even with downtime between to-do items, you can make constant daily progress. It doesn't matter what you say to the world. Nobody cares about your plans, busy schedule, or what holds you back. They may listen out of compassion, love, concern, or obligation while thinking, "*Wow. When will they do something instead of talking about the same d*mn thing.?*" I have lost the capacity to listen to broken records. Action doesn't require you to speak—not one word.

SHUT-UP AND GRIND

Get serious about your life and your goals. If you want to progress, talk less and do more. Learn and adjust as you fight forward; you will improve as you go. How much time do you have to get your stuff done? Opportunities don't wait for you to catch up. Regardless of everything, it's simple: just shut up and grind.

Becoming an expert in any field takes an estimated ten thousand hours. Do you have that amount of time invested in your dream or business? Why not? How about time invested in watching television? Do you know the average person watches about three hours of TV daily? That staggering statistic equates to enough wasted time to become an expert in any field every nine years. Step it up and be more productive—you're not going as hard as you think.

There is no lying to yourself. Speaking of which, in the next chapter, we'll take a closer look at integrity. Personal integrity will help ensure you are on track when pursuing your goals, but overall integrity will ensure you are on the right path in all areas of life.

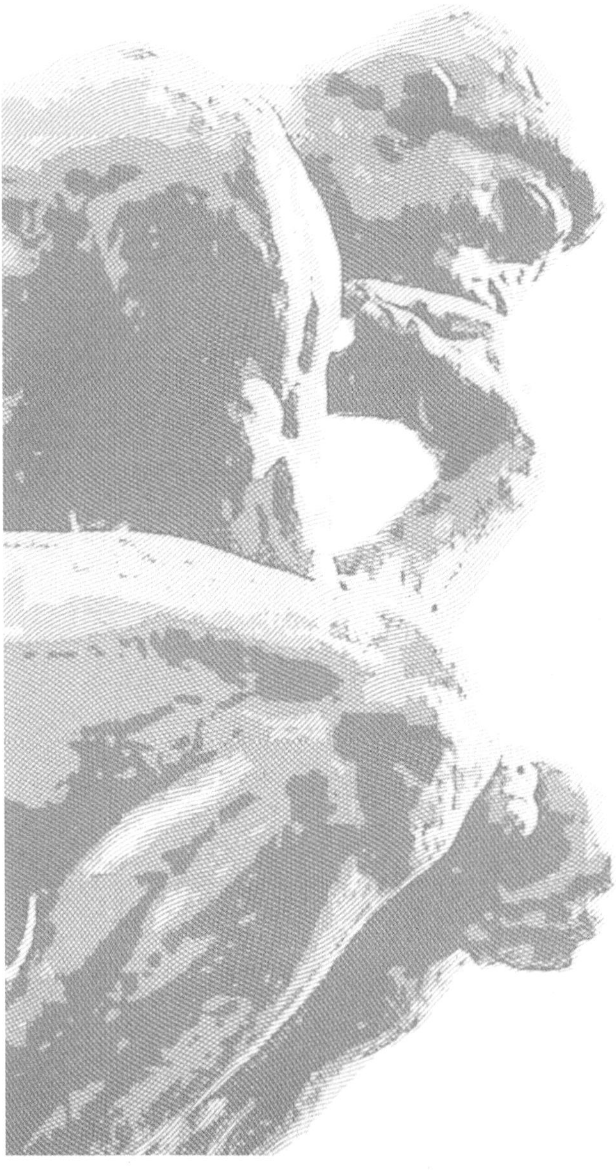

CHAPTER 7

INTEGRITY

> "In matters of style, swim with the current;
> in matters of principle, stand like a rock."
> —Thomas Jefferson[24]

WHY IS INTEGRITY ESSENTIAL FOR BUILDING TRUST AND CREDIBILITY?

I used to think integrity was simply doing the right thing when no one was watching. Well, it is, but that is just a small portion. You don't have to be a saint to want to do what's right based on subjective ethical behavior. The characteristics I strive to continue to develop are closely related to doing what is inherently correct.

I am a fighter with purpose, the protector, and the corrector. My purpose is to inspire, guide, and protect others. I prefer to teach than respond thoughtlessly due to a lack of self-control. Sometimes, it's hard not to; it is like a full-time job not to. Self-control takes a great deal of strength and discipline. Integrity is about being what you consider *a good person*. Have you ever made a mistake and had to apologize to anyone? Of course, we all

---

[24] Thomas Jefferson, "In Matters of Style, Swim with the Current; in Matters of Principle, Stand Like a Rock," BrainyQuote, accessed September 23, 2023, https://www.brainyquote.com/quotes/thomas_jefferson_121032.

have. That is one of the things that makes us human, defined as beings of imperfection.

One winter, after leaving the casino, I dropped about ten grand out of a carry-on book bag, and a friend of mine, the late great David Shaw, found it. At the time, he didn't have much money (which soon changed), and he still called me five minutes after I left and told me I had dropped something. I asked him to keep it until the next day, and he replied, "Nah, I think you might want to come get this real quick." Now, that's what I call integrity. And he proved himself loyal a million times since that day. I wouldn't have known the money was missing, and he did not try to surreptitiously see if I knew it was gone or try to keep it. He just told me he had it. That is one example of integrity I refer to in my life.

> "If you wish to escape moral and physical assassination, do nothing, say nothing, be nothing."
> — Elbert Hubbard[25]

Whether in relationships, missed opportunities, or life in general, your contributions, perceptions, and responses weigh heavily upon your character. You are not officially an adult until you take full responsibility for your actions, which also includes how you respond to others. I don't try to do everything perfectly, but my concentration has been on doing what is morally correct. I wasn't always like this.

Admittedly, it is not always easy, especially when you can benefit; it is something small, or the repercussions are not apparent. "It's not like anybody's going to know," says the little devil on your shoulder, but the world *will* know. Let me explain. When someone is sneaky, they develop an energy that cannot be trusted—a slimy vibe. Those milliseconds of abnormal hesitation at those vital moments under the microscope shine more than

---

[25] Elbert Hubbard, *Little Journeys to the Homes of American Statesmen*, Reprinted (New York: The Knickerbocker Press, 1901), http://hdl.handle.net/2027/hvd.hx4zk6, 370.

anything they have ever done. People begin to say, "It is just something about him; I can't put my finger on it," or "he has bad energy." However, not everyone with bad energy has a slimy vibe. We will touch on this in greater detail in Chapter 10.

WHAT DEFINES INTEGRITY?

Finding trustworthy people is not only challenging; it is nearly impossible. It's like *squeezing water out of a rock*. I am far from perfect. I say what I mean and make decisions I can stand behind. It may seem negligible, but if I believe what you say and your actions and words align, I can trust you, but only over time. Taking additional steps to reinforce your character with the personal accountability required to keep your standards high is what integrity is all about.

It's not what you get by doing and insisting; it is who you become in the process, and the same is true for the opposite. One may not get caught engaging in activities that encompass undesirable elements or negative vibrations, but a person's energy becomes questionable. Do you not think the people you encounter can discern your character? That's who you are. What is done in the dark eventually comes to light. Misrepresentation of self is an attempt to hide in plain sight with a poor disguise.

The tenets of motivation mentioned in these chapters are a few of the elements I use when evaluating situations and deciding whom to associate with. When you have relentless motivation, unclouded vision, a solid plan, and laser-like focus, the only thing left to do is take action and take over the world by force but with integrity.

Next, we will discuss what it takes to push forward, irrespective of negativity or any perceived level of adversity or opposition.

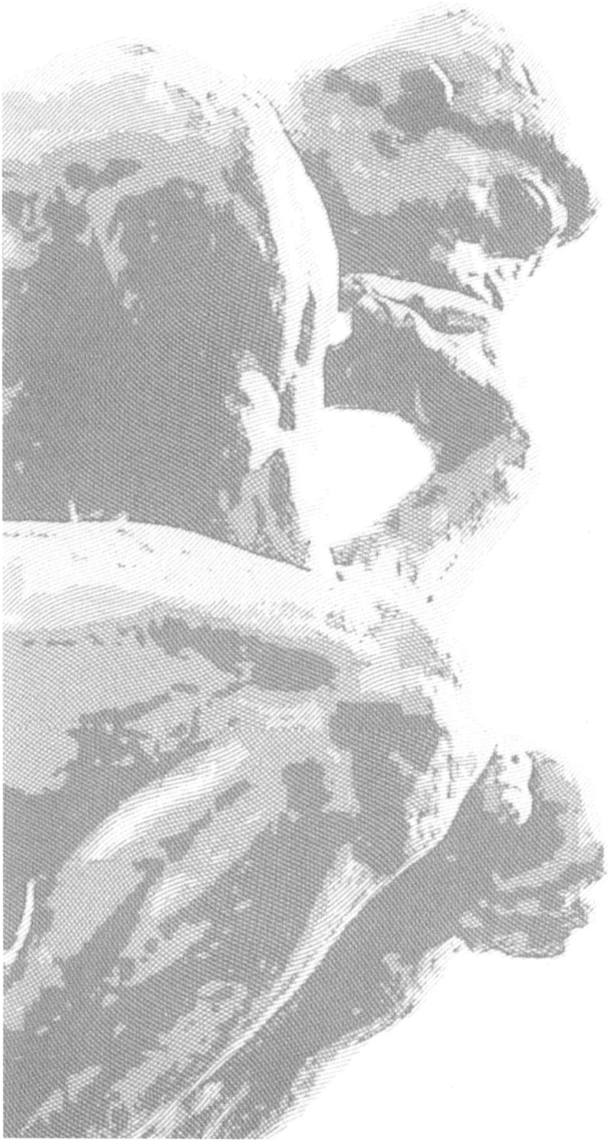

CHAPTER 8

PERSISTENCE

> "The higher a goal a person pursues,
> the quicker his ability develops."
>
> —Maksim Gorky[26]

HOW SHOULD YOU RESPOND WHEN FACING ADVERSITY?

There is a difference between wanting to do something and not stopping until you get it done. This thought process applies when working independently as well as with others.

I view midrange and short-term goals like the legs of a road trip. Let's say you're traveling five hundred miles, which we'll consider a midrange goal. First, you would map out your journey, establishing a solid plan with clear directions. Every hundred miles or so will be what we consider short-term. You would not drive the first hundred miles and let a flat tire, traffic delay, or inclement weather make that random location your final destination unless it was impossible to continue, correct? You would figure it out no

---

[26] Maxim Gorky, "The Higher Goal a Person Pursues, the Quicker His Ability Develops, and the More Beneficial He Will Become to the Societ…," Quotefancy, accessed September 24, 2023, https://quotefancy.com/quote/1057713/Maxim-Gorky-The-higher-goal-a-person-pursues-the-quicker-his-ability-develops-and-the.

matter what because the final destination is your only objective, stopping at nothing short of a successful trip.

This is the same way you should respond in real life. When you set goals and encounter miscellaneous obstacles along the way, don't stop. Instead, quickly pivot and figure out how to keep moving until you achieve your goals. Before you begin anything, plan it out so you have clear directions. Create a checklist to ensure you cover all the bases. Here is the crucial part: Finish strong without getting distracted or deterred.

FORCE YOUR WAY IN

After an overdue vacation, I returned home through Heathrow International Airport in London. If you have ever been there, you know shuffling between terminals is like catching a shuttle to another city. After landing, I realized that my connecting flight was about five minutes away by car, so I proceeded to the bus stop to wait for the shuttle. The driver slowed down to pick me up, but there was no space.

I was about two hundred and ninety pounds of muscle with two carry-ons, so squeezing in seemed impossible. I didn't think of getting in, and as the door slowly began to close, this little fiery white lady said, "There's room; come on!" And everybody backed up. She told me, "Thanks for your service." I remember her saying, "Sometimes you've got to force your way in." Those indelible words stained my memory. *Who did God send to welcome me back to reality?*

Recently, I was walking with my close friend Juju in Virginia Beach at the corner of Twenty-Fourth Street, crossing over Pacific Avenue, headed eastbound toward the oceanfront. When we arrived at the crosswalk, even though pedestrians had the right of way, they were just standing there, waiting for the passing cars to slow down. Guess what? They never did; they just kept moving. The drivers were inconsiderate, but why would they do otherwise with no threat of immediate consequences?

I turned to Juju and said, "I'll make them stop!" She looked at me like I was crazy but stayed by my side because she trusted me. With cars fast approaching, I took the outside lane to shield her from the possibility of an accident. Taking my first step, not looking at the cars, but with my eyes fixed on the other side of the street, I could hear several engines downshift, and we just kept walking. The vehicles stopped because nobody wanted to *hit a pedestrian.* Drivers fear that and proceed with caution when approaching crosswalks, even if they don't appear to slow down.

I was not going to chill and wait for my chance. Instead, I took advantage of the window of opportunity. "Sometimes, you've got to force your way in." Nobody will hand you anything, and sometimes you must skip the line, especially when time is of the essence. And guess what—time is always of the essence. Don't wait! Go hard now and forever. Skip the line, wake people up, cut out the fluff, and jump straight to the point. Sometimes, you just have to say the hell with it, kill the excuses, and do it anyway. When it is hard, tough, painful, uncomfortable, unknown, too heavy, you're sick, don't feel like it, or whatever your excuse, trust me, just do it anyway. There is no growth without resistance and persistence.

ELEVATE

Respect is taken. Think about it. When somebody talks to you like they are crazy and you snap at them with immediate correction, putting them in their place, they look like they have cake on their face and freeze out of shock. Bullies only bully those who don't fight back. Similarly, people only respect those they can't disrespect. Water, electricity, and disrespect all flow in the path of least resistance, so put up a fight. You don't fix problems in the third person. Be direct and speak up immediately.

You must demand that those you deal with show you respect. It is not optional. You must insist, be tough, and stand up for yourself and others. This does not need to be accomplished disrespectfully but focus on achieving your primary objective and getting your point across. Why go through the hassle of anything without accomplishing your mission? You could have made more progress doing nothing.

Let the words fly if your only objective is to speak your mind. But if you intend to gain understanding and improve processes and relationships, you must have a clear understanding and communication. When it comes to your needs and requirements, both in business and in your personal life, be both rigidly flexible and persistent. Instead of matching energy, aim to elevate it!

We are not concentrating on one area. This broad topic multilaterally applies to finances, education, self-improvement, relationships, communication, spirituality, and goals. We must insist in every aspect of our lives. Don't get distracted, and don't take no for an answer. We often become preoccupied by emotionally fixating on irresolute issues, which alter our perspective and make negotiating more difficult. It limits our ability to listen actively, think consciously, and respond appropriately.

SELF-INFLICTED WOUNDS

One evening before dinner, while on base overseas, I arrived hungry as hell at the crowded mess hall where everybody contended for parking spaces, especially for Friday's Surf-n-Turf. A few seconds after securing my truck's position, the commander of the British Army aggressively approached me, wearing a maroon beret, with his two bodyguards at his side. Somewhere between his tirade over a stolen parking space and attempting to berate me for not calling him sir, he called me a f*cking American as if it was an insult. I stayed outside in isolation for a few minutes to practice some of the techniques that I learned in anger management. I stood still, slowly counting to ten while taking deep breaths and pausing before exhaling. I couldn't decide if the exercise was calming my mind or only pissing me off by delaying my response and intensifying my thoughts of the recent incident.

I decided that his intended disrespect was intolerable, and the unknown ramifications of my immediate actions were worth the risk of termination and a few days in jail. I didn't want to kill him; I would settle for humiliation. I marched into the cafeteria, entering through the exit, and saw the vulnerable commander laughing and eating with his guards still at his side. He didn't notice as I approached, further enraged by their smiling faces—

and then it happened. I backhand slapped him with so much force that he flew sideways, but his body rolled forward, leaving him seizing and convulsing under the bench-style dining room table.

He pissed himself, suffering a broken, bloody nose. After I interrupted his meal with physical on-the-spot correction, his bodyguards swiftly moved into an attack position but did not advance toward my aggressive defensive posture. The military police stated that they heard the slap from outside. Three US Army commanders quickly intervened to de-escalate, but not fast enough to prevent the slap. My fall from grace was worth his embarrassment. As the military police walked me outside, the ambient background noise from the hundreds of US soldiers transitioned from complete silence to a low, thunderous roar with a celebrative undertone. I returned to work the following morning.

> **Key Takeaway:** Maintaining self-control under duress can enhance your focus and ability to make wise conscious decisions.

We have established that we are not taking no for an answer and demanding what we require, but we must give credit to our team and those who help us create our visions.

From birth to our last breath, we are a symbiotic community. Life is in balanced harmony when we hinge our strengths together as one working machine.

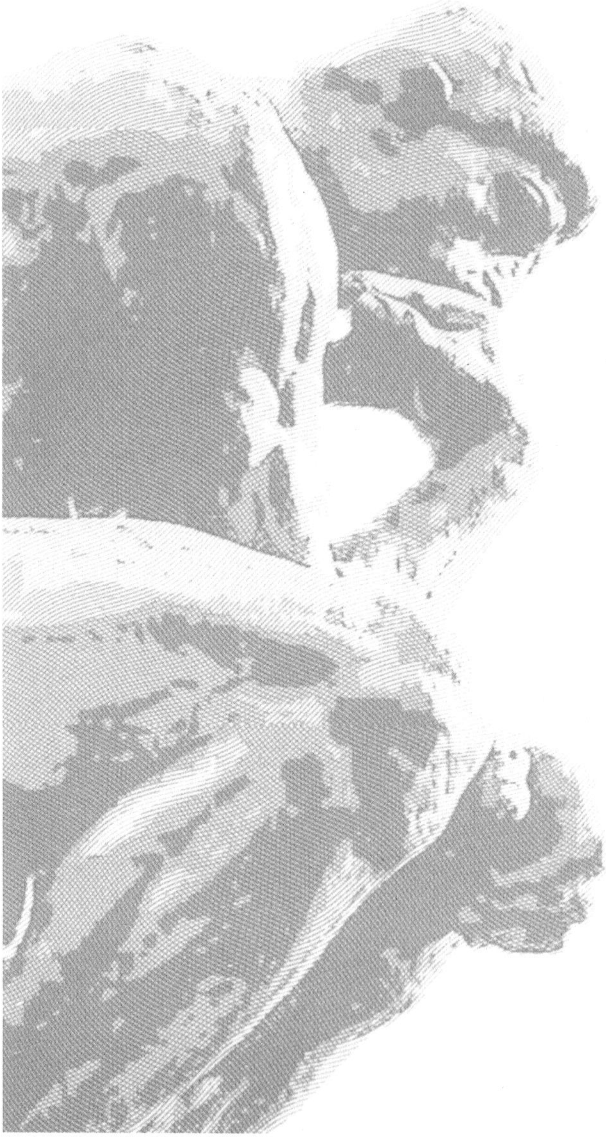

CHAPTER 9

INTERDEPENDENCE

> "If I have seen further, it is by standing on the shoulders of giants."
>
> —Isaac Newton[27]

HAVE YOU TRIED TAPPING INTO THE POWER OF THE ALLIANCES YOU CREATED WITHIN YOUR NETWORK?

Interdependence is two or more autonomous forces aligning toward a common goal or set of objectives. Through interdependence, self-sustaining entities can synergistically collaborate by effectively leveraging strengths and complementing each other's weaknesses to achieve elevated levels of focused productivity—the epitome of getting stuff done as a team.

I am the creator, strategist, and inventor. Once I develop a great idea, I have a team with the skillsets necessary to help reach the next level. Now, I can make great strides of progress without the help of anyone; however, with the assistance of an expert search engine optimizer and marketer, I can quickly bring my ideas to market, which is an example of interdependence. If you can effectively network with independent resources that support your cause (and you also support theirs),

---

[27] Isaac Newton, "If I Have Seen Further Than Others, It Is by Standing Upon the Shoulders of Giants," BrainyQuote, accessed September 24, 2023, https://www.brainyquote.com/quotes/isaac_newton_135885.

you can master interdependence. Focus on adding value and being as efficient as possible in your area of responsibility, and you will become an irreplaceable asset and an ideal team member.

Find people as focused and motivated as you with the skills and abilities to catapult your ideas, optimize your business, and help your dreams become a reality. Make sure you choose the right people. Be open-minded. Surround yourself with people on the same mission as you with similar skills who can operate autonomously without each other but work better together because of what they bring to the table.

Let's analyze the United States military. We have several branches with different responsibilities. There are also countless roles within each branch, all seamlessly working together to achieve one thing: global superiority. Now, one mission may be to put bombs on target, but there are millions of elements of tactically intertwined multifaceted parameters that are significant stand-alone assets but unstoppable when combined and executed in tandem.

When I deployed to southern Iraq in 2006, I didn't know why we were fighting the war at the time. We all remain unsure of how we selected our ill-advised targets in retaliation to the deplorable September 11th attacks based on the media's conflated portrayal of the invasion of Iraq. All I knew was that about a thousand of our men and women were killed in action at the beginning of 2006, and I owed it to my country to get off my ass and get over there and contribute. I got picked up by a great company that shall remain anonymous. After two days in Baghdad, I was quickly promoted and flown off as the southern Iraq Site Lead for the counter radio-controlled improvised explosive device electronic warfare system program.

Regardless of how you currently view war, your perspective is about to change and hopefully improve. I previously viewed war as several tactics and strategies orchestrated and executed simultaneously to accomplish a set of objectives. I also saw war as one branch of service or several synchronized branches working together but all from the same country. But what I soon learned shaped a new world of operations that I was beyond fortunate to support.

The enemy was relentless, so there were constantly emerging threats to interpret, learn to navigate, minimize, and eliminate. We were offensively defensive while engaging in a real-time version of 3-D chess, where all the pieces were constantly changing, upgraded, or invisible. Other than the numerous branches of US forces present, there was also a high presence of UN (United Nations) coalition support forces.

Everyone had a different role. Some constantly checked the Main Supply Route for explosives, while others hunted for snipers. Each country had a different mission and provided an increased capability, all of which helped achieve the ultimate, long-term objective of ground superiority while minimizing the threat of IEDs to get supplies to those in need. This coordination was orchestrated by the commanding generals in the United States, analyzing data and strategizing while maintaining constant communication and coordinating with the forward-deployed commanders. I viewed this as a new level of teamwork. Several highly advanced self-sustaining organizations came together in support of a common cause. The assembly of this coalition was technical mastery and interdependence, which is how it should be in life and business.

Disparity

If I'm going as hard as I can, and so are you, it won't matter what our shortcomings are because we'd appreciate the effort and support each other. Problems will arise when one side is not pulling its weight. I'm not getting my fair share if we receive an equal split, but I am putting in more effort. Most people find it difficult to express their concerns in a way that will be well-received. It is an emotional topic, primarily because when you decide to speak up, it will cause a misunderstanding because of the tone explosion, which is the perfect catalyst for an argument.

I can tell you how to avoid this, but the solution may be apparent. My recommendation: speak up as soon as possible. Ensure you clearly define individual roles and responsibilities as they correspond to achieving each overall team objective. If you have individuals on your team with a growth mindset, they will embrace innovative ideas and constructive criticism. If they resist and respond with irrelevant points of contention, they may have to develop more in terms of self-awareness and social understanding. We all have areas in which we need to improve. Most communication issues are derived from misunderstandings. Be clear, direct, and honest. Not speaking up is the only failure when seeking or providing clarity.

Notwithstanding the mission, this concept still applies. I have seen several influencers on social media tell the world that they are doing everything as solopreneurs while still pushing their sales pitch on social media to grow their network in hopes of obtaining new leads and converting those leads into sales. I am not saying they are full of it. They obviously need somebody, right?

You could be the most extraordinary businessperson in the world, and even if you can strategize and set up everything by yourself, you will be much more efficient with the assistance of leveraged resources. There is an advertising agency that can do a much better job at getting customers to engage with your content, support your business, and buy your products. Imagine hiring them to take care of your ads, marketing, promotions, and sales, freeing you to focus solely on your product selection, growth, and numbers so the result reflects your best.

Who is the best player in the world? Do they play a team sport? They would be unknown without the right support system. It takes a team, and we all need help sometimes. Just think: what if Michael Jordan never played professionally, but he practiced every day? He would be a nobody in the NBA world of basketball or one of the many college greats we seem to have slowly forgotten. I am making this point: there is strength and emotional intelligence in doing as much as possible for yourself but also knowing when to team up. The concept to keep in mind is to get the job done in the most efficient manner possible.

Resource Selection

Get moving with a team in place or at least a list of those who can assist in your journey. That idea that you have in the vault has been there for who knows how long—it barely has a pulse, and it is urgent that you get it done immediately, if not sooner, or it will never happen. If you aren't doing it now, *chances are you never will*.

If you focus and lay out all the pieces of your plan, you can align the most appropriate resources with what you need to accomplish while maximizing your performance and efficiency. Regardless of how good you are, you can invariably improve, and no matter what you think you know, you can always learn more. Selecting talented subject matter experts as your team members is just one piece of the puzzle.

The other question you must ask is, what type of people are they? Do they have to be passionate to be effective? How do you feel when you are around them and vice versa? The same goes for you. What kind of person are you? Why do people come to you? What type of conversations do you have? Are you talking about ideas and plans (growth), or is it all politics and people (trash)? This says a lot about you, maybe more than you know.

You create the future you want to live in, and it starts with your mindset and attitude, much of which is reflected through conversation and nonverbal cues, such as body language. Other aspects of judgment may appear as prescience or foresight; however, if you learn to trust and listen to your gut, you may detect other valuable attributes or indications that you can use to your advantage, especially in conscious decision-making.

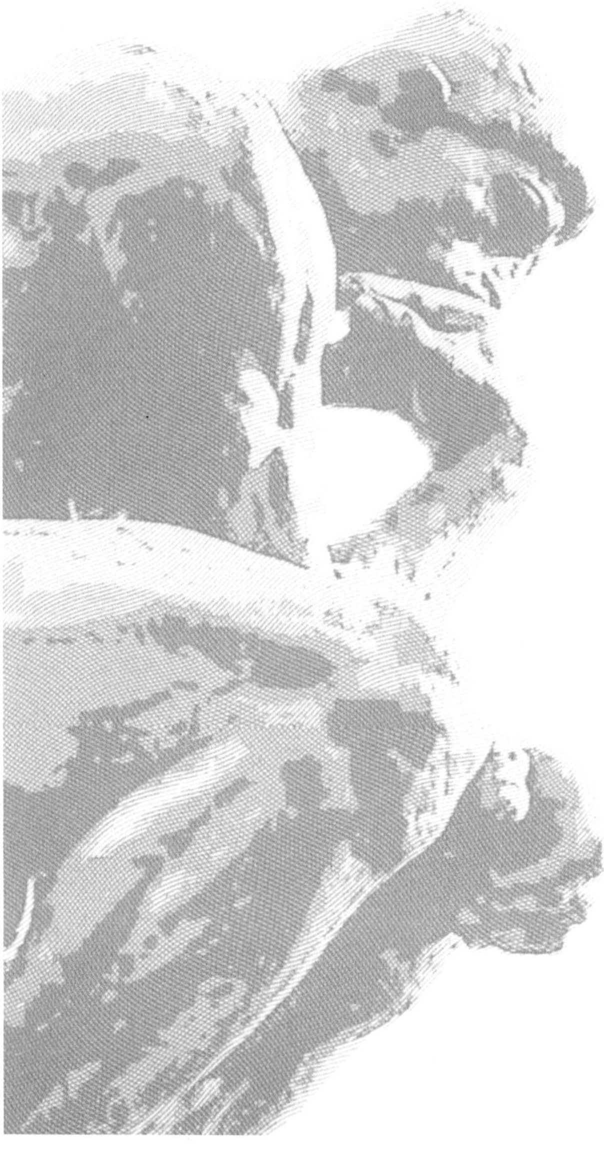

Chapter 10

Energy, Instinct, and Intuition

> "Have the courage to follow your heart and intuition. They somehow already know what you truly want to become."
> —Steve Jobs[28]

Do you trust your instincts and ability to leverage your intuition to assist you in making critical decisions?

The energy you receive and emanate directly correlates to your mood and level of motivation. Learning to control your influences can help you maintain focused mental clarity while remaining unaffected by nonsense, navigating your thoughts, and making better decisions.

Energy

Some people wake up grateful, excited about life, and ready for anything the world throws at them. You can feel their aura as soon as they walk into a room. I am one of those people.

---

[28] Stanford, "Steve Jobs' 2005 Stanford Commencement Address," Youtube, March 7, 2008, video, 15:04, https://youtu.be/UF8uR6Z6KLc?si=_UV7lemCgWsHdMWN.

REFLECTION

What type of energy do you have? How would people describe you? Would they depict you as a person who is pleasant to be around? Here is another question: How would you characterize the people you spend the most time with? Take your closest friend. Do they smile often? How about when they are silent? Are they calm, or is their energy erratic, tense, and uncomfortable? If you have never thought about their energy, how their vibrations impact you is unclear. However, it doesn't matter if you are accustomed to spending time with someone or if they are strangers; you can tell a lot about anyone through brief interaction and general observation.

It is crucial that you continue to practice the art of reading energy. Regardless of the innumerable events occurring in any given situation, due to confirmation bias, you will only perceive what you reflect or want to see. When you're around, working with, or teaming up with others, understand that their energy will significantly impact yours. This long-term aspect of their character is not subject to change, so pay close attention.

> "Stay away from negative people. They have a problem for every solution."
> —Albert Einstein[29]

INTUITION

Calm your mind and trust your gut. Thoughts cause emotions. Remember the last time you received a call from someone anxious and panicking? They told you it was urgent! They were almost out of breath and difficult to understand while attempting to tell you what was happening. They didn't ask you if you had a minute. They just jumped in and told you

---

[29] Andy Murphy, "A Reason to Stay Away from Negative People (According to Albert Einstein)," Medium, July 19, 2022, https://medium.com/writers-blokke/a-reason-to-stay-away-from-negative-people-according-to-albert-einstein-9139189166a.

about their emergency, based on the worst-case scenario, requiring your immediate attention. The first law of nature is self-preservation.

This law applies to you and those you love, and I'm sure you stopped everything because you were willing to save the day. However, did you slow down to ask yourself how you thought you should respond and how you truly felt? Or did you immediately believe the conjecture and react based on the presented information? Perhaps you sensed that the outcome would return favorable results, and maybe they were overreacting.

In the future, try this: Eliminate your emotional responses; pause for a moment, breathe, and pay closer attention to how you feel and what you think. You will notice all of your senses concertedly attune to your most prevalent thoughts. I typically apply this concept to feelings of uneasiness, but recently, I also recognize when I am abnormally at peace with whatever the outcome may be and have a resounding inclination that the result will be favorable. This type of thinking also reduces situational anxiety. It is different from not caring or going with the flow.

I can tell the difference between what my mind amplifies (the emergency) and my intuition, which helps me make smarter decisions. I am always aware of my thoughts, but my intuition has precedence over influencing my choices and decisions, especially when dealing with others. Trusting intuition will help sharpen your sixth sense and improve your decision-making process. You may put the perfect plan on pause if you get a weird feeling or—capitalize on a brief opportunity you would have otherwise missed, which will also help you practice mindfulness and patience while mastering the art of timing.

I have been in a few situations where things did not feel right, causing me to adjust my plans accordingly. I'm not talking about being nervous or anxious; I'm talking about that weird out-of-the-blue "let me get off of this plane, catch another taxi, look both ways, no second date for her, don't trust him, he's just a salesman, maybe I should circle the block or call first if I have to take my gun, maybe I shouldn't go, or if I do, take an extra clip" feeling. I am talking about what stimulates your intuition. Ignoring these indicators will only lead to regret, lost time, or worse. I recall an inconceivable instance where ignoring these signs could have ended in catastrophe with multiple casualties.

I am notorious for speeding. I received three concurrent speeding tickets in 2003 (while driving the silver bullet) for going 109-mph in a 55-mph zone, almost double the speed limit. The trooper said he chased me through three counties and asked if I knew how fast I was going. Without hesitation, I replied honestly, "It depends on how long you were following me." I lost my license due to this incident but had received another license in an adjacent state before revocation, so I maintained my privileges. I felt fortunate that I didn't get clocked while doing 160-mph about five minutes earlier. If I was ever challenged while behind the wheel, I often accepted. It was almost like an automatic reaction.

However, this one time, I was on my way to Atlanta for a meeting on Halloween in 2009, and while in a deep conversation with "D," we both witnessed a car fly past us. Let me pause and point out that I was in a 75-mph zone and doing my version of the speed limit with cruise control at fourteen over. When the car passed, D asked, "You see that?" and we laughed. My initial thought was to give chase, catch up, and leave them in the dust, but oddly, I did something I never did concerning speed. Even though I knew I could get away with it—not a trooper in sight or on the radar detector—I had a strange feeling and decided to ignore them, relax, and drive. The same car passed us again. They flew by, slowed down to taunt us, and took off even faster.

But what happened next was mortifying and life-changing. When the vehicle flew by the second time, it was going at least 120-mph because it passed us like we were sitting in a parked car. It had our undivided attention at this point—and then it happened. The black coupe began to fishtail from left to right about three or four times, and then suddenly, it almost shot over the bridge; luckily, the guardrails were in place. The car stood up on its grill as it spun wildly, and then smoke and sparks shot down the highway ahead of the mangled vehicle that followed. I swear the car tumbled at least fifty yards. As we observed, we witnessed what we thought were two bumpers hurling through the air. We jumped out to offer assistance. Time was of the essence because their car was smoking and beginning to catch fire. We could see someone trapped in the vehicle, so we forced open the door and pulled the young man to safety.

Like in the movies, as soon as we got the person safely removed from the vehicle, the car engulfed in flames. The objects that were thought to be bumpers were later confirmed as two individuals: a small girl with minor bruises and a young man named Jesse, who sadly had no pulse and sustained severe head injuries. He, unfortunately, did not survive the incident. I gave a full account of what I saw to the authorities and, a few days later, spoke with his mother, Cheryl, about what I observed, omitting the graphic details out of respect for his memory. I was accustomed to accelerating at speeds well above that of the coupe and I feel incredibly fortunate that I did not respond to the challenge and listened to my gut. Still, I hate that someone lost their life.

SPIRITUALITY

Spirituality is the understanding, study, or belief in a power or force that exists in an unobservable dimension that correlates, be it direct or indirect, with our existence through religion, our psyche, our inner self, or other incomprehensible factors beyond our control.

DESTINED FOR GREATNESS

I mentioned spirituality and other concepts as a reminder of your greatness. Your value far exceeds anything material. It is impossible to grasp an all-encompassing deity's imperceivable magnitude and power; however, there is evidence of God presented in many forms. Everything that has life reflects this power, and with this potential, what we focus on, we also create. But where is the confusion? The issue is the intentional creation of division through religion. The only understanding I see congruent in all religions is the "my God is the only God" mentality, which is an absolute truth, but until you understand that your God is also in you, you will remain confused about who you are within our macrocosm, your purpose, and your incalculable capability, power, and strength.

TAPPING-IN

It was a typical 90-degree summer Saturday. I was nineteen years old, at my first duty station, with no plans for the evening. I had finished eating and was about to leave the base to head home and relax. Life was simple, and I was going with the flow when I ran into Brian Rampy, whom I had met in basic training. He was smart, laid back, and quiet. He mastered blending in with the background and was cool to hang out with. Immediately, I could tell he was going out because he was dressed like he was going to the prom, with creased jeans and a sharp black button-up.

He asked me if I wanted to go to a bar to enjoy the dancers. I thought, "Hell yeah," but I had a strange, unexplainable gut feeling. It was like the DJ suddenly cut the music. Time appeared to slow down, and I can still remember the expression on his face. Sadly, that was the last time I saw him alive.

When I returned to work the following Monday, Master Sergeant Brogan, the shop chief, informed everyone of Brian's passing. While leaving the bar, he fell asleep behind the wheel before attempting to cross a bridge and did not survive the accident. Upon request, I honorably escorted him home from Seymour Johnson Air Force Base in North Carolina to return him to his Texas home to his parents, Edwin, and Nora Rampy, who welcomed me with open arms. They both called me their son, which I will never forget. Losing Brian was a tragedy. He was a good brother.

BRINGING IT ALL TOGETHER

Do I feel responsible? No. But I wish I had told him about the weird feeling, even though I didn't understand it. Maybe it would've saved his life. I have never revealed the details of this incident to anyone until now. This occurrence was the first time I experienced an uncommon feeling that provided a resounding understanding of how it could've affected me, had I not acknowledged my intuition and responded accordingly. Hearing news or thinking about a situation, my emotions give me a pretty accurate indication of the future outcome. I don't know how this is possible without additional insight or influence that may impact the result. Until now, I haven't been that interested in researching the topic, but I proceed with the understanding that there are powerful forces beyond our awareness and comprehension that we routinely encounter.

If you continue listening to your gut and learn to trust your intuition, you can view events clearly while evaluating realistic possibilities. Practice remaining calm when making decisions; it will be easier to differentiate fear from reality. I'm not speaking of scarcely credible psychic abilities but about trusting your judgement and intuition when making conscious decisions. When something doesn't feel right, it usually isn't. There may be no noticeable signs or anomalous errors, but you know something's amiss.

Moreover, there's evidence of existential relationships in the quantum realm that we are only at the precipice of understanding. There are books written based on countless hours of research, yet we know little about many of the complex relationships that exist in this world. Even the most intelligent humans to ever walk the earth were elementary at best in their understanding of the power we possess and how we are all spiritually and metaphysically connected. Our intelligence is limited (as we know it). There is a lot of information we can't grasp about our minds, the world around us, or even the air we breathe, so we lack the intellectual capacity required to develop a comprehensive understanding of the correlation between nonmaterial elements.

All that spiritual/metaphysical and transcendental stuff can be a little much. Still, I believe in vibrations, synchronicities, karma, auras, manifestations, and intuition. If you don't, it doesn't matter; still, I'm sure you've felt weird vibes you can't explain, so that may be something to think about.

I understand with absolute certainty that effort performance, energy, and vibrations can positively or adversely affect any outcome. Your intuition, emotions, and conscious thoughts assist you during your decision-making process, and knowing who you are and why you are on your chosen path will contribute to your discernment and overall understanding. I have no idea how I made it this far in life without being able to detect subtle cues for so long, but I know where I give all the credit.

If I were to write a letter to my younger self, it would be:

John-Boy,

"What's up, champ? There are so many things I could teach you, but time and personal experience will provide all the answers when you are ready to receive them. Always believe in yourself and chase your dreams; you will do more and go further than you could ever imagine. Keep trying different things because this will show you how smart and resilient you are. You will meet some amazing people, and some will be lucky enough to stay in your life. Make sure you stay close to your baby sister because, as her older brother, it is your responsibility to protect her and be a loyal friend.

But do yourself a favor—figure people out as soon as possible. Keep your distance if they don't show that they love and want you around. It doesn't matter why. You have a big personality, a lot of energy, and a very bright future. Just do what makes you happy and be around the people who bring out the best in you. Also, do not spend too much time on religion; just know that God is very real. You will figure the rest out. Go slow and remember that time is on your side. You will grow up and be something like an unstoppable force. Anything you focus on will come to fruition, so what should you do with that information? Exactly. Focus on what you want to do, control your influences, trust your intuition, and chase your dreams!

WE HAVE THE POWER

The major takeaway from this chapter is this: Trust yourself, continue to take your time, remain focused, and believe in your abilities. You have a power far greater than you know. Do not be distracted by someone's malignant psychological manipulation to utilize your focus, energy, and time for their benefit. Spend time concentrating on the thoughts that contribute to your vision. Believe that you can accomplish your objectives and let your motivation turn to action, then watch mountains start to move.

While perfecting your plan and getting things done, be mindful of your energy and those around you. Once you define your why and remove every excuse to maintain the course with the focused impetus required to push forward, there is only one thing to concentrate on: your follow-through. What is the point of investing money, time, and energy in anything if you don't dedicate as much focus and attention to completion? Time is so precious that going off half-cocked, and not seeing your plans through to the end is an atrocity.

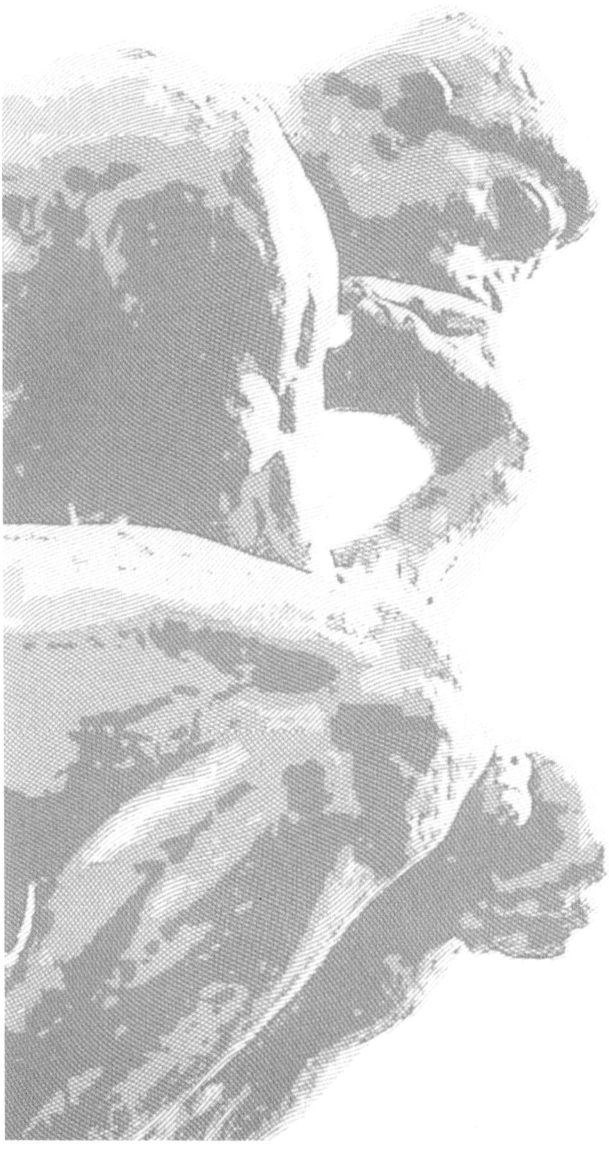

CHAPTER 11

CHECKMATE: ENDGAME

"Look to the future because that is
where you'll spend the rest of your life."

—George Burns[30]

IS IT A DESIGN FLAW TO DEVELOP A STRATEGY WITHOUT FIRST CONSIDERING THE ANTICIPATED OUTCOME?

No matter what you're doing or how bulletproof your plan is, you will make mistakes, but everything you have read so far will help ensure you're prepared for the challenges you will face in the future. All remarkable things take time, so pace yourself.

DO NOT RELENT

I have an uncle (Abu Muhammad Saleem) who is close in age to my father. My uncle would probably like to remain anonymous, but he deserves a mention, nonetheless. I told him about my plans and lofty aspirations a few years ago. I do not remember much from the conversation. What I do remember, though, are his three words of advice. After I told him what was

---

[30] George Burns, "I Look to the Future Because That's Where I'm Going to Spend the Rest of My Life," BrainyQuote, accessed September 24, 2023, https://www.brainyquote.com/quotes/george_burns_189717.

on my mind, he took a deep breath, sat up straighter, paused for his usual three or four seconds, and then replied, <u>"Do not relent."</u>

It was impossible for him to know how focused, determined, and impenetrable my mind is due to how infrequently we communicate; however, it was great advice—especially from someone who watched me grow up, who (like my father) strives for moral perfection. If you are trying different things, once you realize a venture doesn't suit you, it's perfectly fine to stop. Go slow, take calculated risks, and cut your losses early. But let's focus on the topic at hand: Finishing strong.

It is encouraging to look at it like this. Most entrepreneurs may not know much about business, but that doesn't stop them from jumping headfirst, hoping to eventually figure things out. Do you know why that is? Because they are focused on the results they want to achieve. Even if their plan is elementary at best, the result is the priority. That says a lot. If you are myopic, the finish line can disappear, especially when you're distracted. Focus on completion.

THAT'S MATE!

I wanted to learn how the pieces moved when I started playing chess, which is also similar to the collective response you will receive from seasoned veterans if you challenge them to a meeting of the minds. They comfortably disarm potential victims by introducing their intentions as nonthreatening. Before ascending to my current level and rating, I played smart but lacked one thing. I never thought about the checkmate until the latter part of the game. I would get so excited about developing complicated attacks that I would forget about the endgame. My moves left me on the opposing side of the opponent's king, which led me to make unnecessary sacrifices to regain the calculated advantage that I should have never relinquished. Most of the time, I lost those games, during which I got frustrated due to costly mistakes.

Even so, this 1,500-year-old pastime quickly became my favorite when I learned how to play, especially after I understood the significance of strategy, not just moving pieces. I started mastering openings, pins, forks, and releases. I got good enough to read and dictate moves. This allowed me to begin to see from the perspective of the grandmasters. For instance, during imminent development, telltale signs of an opponent's intentions become readily apparent the more you play and study the game. Certain moves begin to flow instinctively. I even annotated a few rules of my own. For instance, I never put my king and queen in the same line of fire or on the same color squares—an effortless way to lose a queen to a power piece or a protected pawn.

There are also several openings—from aggressive attacks to impenetrable defenses. Memorizing these openings can help you attack early and thwart vicious assailants. During these exchanges, be careful because there are several lethal combinations, unforeseen moves, miscalculations, and even sacrifices.

Regardless of what occurs and where you are left, mathematically, at the end of any piece exchange, every move you make should be aligned with one goal: the endgame—checkmate. Objectively, every decision should be based on logical execution, and the sharper your vision into the future and the broader your perception of eminent envelopment, the stronger your game will be. This holds true when evaluating chess moves and navigating life.

"It's not how hard you pushed along the way. It's having something in you to finish."

—Michael Jordan[31]

WHAT'S NEXT?

For anyone starting a new venture, begin with an end in mind. As you progress, periodically ask yourself, *And then what?* You will begin to see several moves ahead. Most people never think beyond graduating, getting a job, or finishing college. This type of thinking reflects an extreme lack of

---

[31] Michael Jordan, "It's Not How Hard You Pushed Along the Way. It's Having Something in You to Finish." Quotefancy, accessed September 24, 2023, https://quotefancy.com/quote/867570/Michael-Jordan-It-s-not-how-hard-you-pushed-along-the-way-It-s-having-something-in-you-to.

ambition or forethought. I am not saying go into isolation, meditate, write everything down, and question every life decision. Go with the flow if you must, but the question remains: *what's next?* You may decide that is the ultimate objective. There is nothing wrong with that. I applaud it. Because as soon as you achieve your desired result, if you are motivated and driven, you will do nothing but pick another goal and work toward it until you achieve it.

Every move or tactic, series of actions/strategies, or combination thereof is to help you achieve a positional advantage. But what is the purpose of your positional advantage? Am I being too vague? Allow me to clarify. Let's say you land a job making a few hundred thousand dollars a year. What is the purpose of making money if you do nothing but blow it? It is enough to pay your bills, secure a decent mortgage, and drive anything you want. Food, clothes, jewelry, trips, all that stuff is nothing, and you will not appreciate it because you can afford it, so it is just a useless accumulation of things.

Also, did you work so hard to put yourself in that "position" just to buy a several items of material value? Or is there a higher purpose? Are you working so you eventually don't have to work? Are you building generational wealth? Are you establishing multiple streams of income? Is your purpose to teach, motivate, and inspire? Most people say they just want to make more money. But if you make money only to spend it, you could have made the same progress by doing nothing.

Finishing strong is an attitude of trusting your abilities. It is believing in yourself and knowing that you can do anything! Don't just think about it. Have the courage and determination to see your plans through. When I did not know what to do in any given situation on the chessboard, it made me analyze how I was in life. I started considering strategic planning, took a step back, and reevaluated my influences. I immediately got rid of those distractions and took control.

While the mindset of someone moving in this manner may seem advanced, it is what adult thinking looks like. I don't stop, regardless of what occurs, because things will happen. In the same way, I got frustrated with miscalculations or unforeseen circumstances. It happens to everyone, irrespective of skill level. A solid, forward-looking plan is a powerful tool, especially when you are willing to adjust and begin with the end in mind. That means thinking many moves ahead and remaining focused on the outcome.

"To finish first, you must first finish!"

—Juan Manuel Fangio[32]

REALITY CHECK

If you've started anything you're serious about, you should see your plans through to the end. Otherwise, you're just wasting time. If you're not serious and just talking, maybe it feels good to vent. Perhaps you had no idea how much effort was required, and the idea is amazing, but the dedication of time and energy is not attractive. Consider this a reality check. Who are you, and what are you made of? You must dig deep and devote your time and attention to completion, no matter what, or—be honest. Maybe you have a phenomenal idea but decided that it's not worth the effort.

From here on out, don't put effort into anything unless you first plan and dedicate the time and attention required to finish. This preparation will prevent you from going off half-cocked. You may have state-of-the-art weaponry, a fully loaded clip, an extra magazine, a Vortex tactical scope, and great aim with the precision of an eagle's eye. Still, the wrong weapon will never reach the target or make an impact. Failing to perform these initial calculations will only result in disaster. Finishing will take everything mentioned in each chapter of this book, plus the desire and determination to see your goals through to completion. *Do not relent!*

---

[32] Lynn Hidy, "To Finish First, You Must First Finish," *Inside Sales Leadership Corner* (blog), UpYourTelesales, June 7, 2021, https://www.upyourtelesales.com/2021/06/07/to-finish-first-you-must-first-finish/.

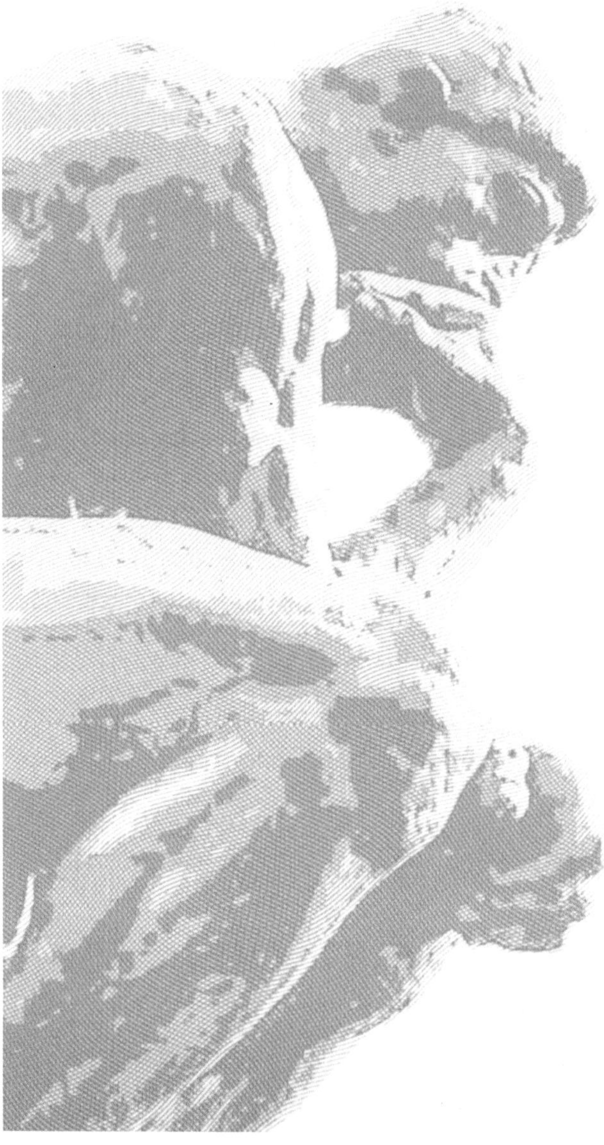

Chapter 12

REFINED CHARACTER

> "Leadership is a potent combination of strategy and character. But if you must be without one, be without the strategy."
>
> —Norman Schwarzkopf [33]

The journey of self-improvement is never-ending and pursuing success requires consistent effort in all areas. This book explored topics related to motivation, discipline, focus, work ethic, strategy, execution, integrity, persistence, interdependence, energy, instinct, intuition, and spirituality.

It is essential to note that achieving success is not a one-size-fits-all approach, and what works for one person may not work for another. Therefore, it's crucial to discover your unique strengths and weaknesses and develop a customized plan that revolves around leveraging your capabilities.

Another aspect of success explored is the importance of balance. Success is not just about achieving professional goals but also about balance and

---

[33] James Kerr, "5 Reasons True Leadership Is All About Character," Inc., February 1, 2016, https://www.inc.com/james-kerr/leadership-in-a-nutshell.html.

fulfillment in your life. It involves taking care of yourself physically, mentally, emotionally, and spiritually and investing in relationships that matter.

> "Success is a path, not a destination."
> —Ashe[34]

One of the most significant takeaways conveyed in this book is that success is not a destination but a journey that requires constant effort, learning, and willingness to grow. Success is not about the impossibility of achieving perfection but progressing toward your goals and continuous improvement.

WHAT'S AHEAD

The journey of self-improvement can be challenging and uncomfortable. It requires you to step outside of your comfort zone and take risks. However, it is essential to remember that failure is a natural part of the journey. Overcoming failures and setbacks propels us to make our most significant advances, so continue to learn from your experiences.

> "If there is a silver lining to bad times, it is this: When facing severe challenges, your mind is normally at its sharpest."
> —Jon Huntsman Sr.[35]

---

[34] Arthur Ashe, "Success Is a Journey, Not a Destination. The Doing Is Often More Important Than the Outcome," BrainyQuote, accessed September 24, 2023, https://www.brainyquote.com/quotes/arthur_ashe_371528.

[35] Jon M. Huntsman, *Winners Never Cheat: Even in Difficult Times*, Revised edition (Upper Saddle River, New Jersey: Pearson Education, 2014), https://ptgmedia.pearsoncmg.com/images/9780137009039/samplepages/9780137009039.pdf, 6.

Throughout these chapters, the central theme is the transformation of a warrior mentality into a refined character. A warrior mentality requires a relentless pursuit of your goals and a willingness to overcome obstacles through sheer determination. Developing a refined character demands that you possess a powerful sense of purpose. Knowing your purpose helps you understand your values, passions, and goals and align them with a sense of meaning and fulfillment.

Clear objectives and self-confidence are essential for establishing your motivation and providing direction and clarity about your goal, allowing you to tap into your full potential and positively impact the world.

THE BIG PICTURE

Developing a refined character involves cultivating emotional intelligence, which includes recognizing and managing your emotions and the emotions of others. It is essential for building strong relationships and effective personal and professional communication, empathizing, building trust, and developing a sense of community. The development of these concepts becomes self-evident as we recap each chapter of the book.

Chapter 1 teaches how a warrior mentality can help us take advantage of and create opportunities. A warrior mentality involves being tough, taking initiative, seeking opportunities, and possessing a mindset of abundance rather than scarcity. However, refining this mentality into a more comprehensive approach that encompasses success, personal growth, and a sense of purpose becomes necessary as you progress.

A warrior mentality can be incredibly beneficial for achieving success but can also lead to burnout and stress without the ideal implementation of a solid work-life balance. Taking breaks and cultivating gratitude and appreciation for your accomplishments is essential.

In **Chapter 2,** we explored the importance of discipline in achieving success. Discipline involves doing what is necessary, even when uncomfortable or inconvenient. It is practicing consistency and mastering the ability to make short-term sacrifices for long-term gains. However, discipline is about structure, self-control, and building character.

Discipline must also balance rigid flexibility and extreme adaptability. Unexpected events have the propensity to throw us off course, and life is unpredictable. Preparing for and adapting to unforeseen and challenging circumstances is necessary, with change being the only constant. Being open to innovative ideas and approaches and pivoting when necessary are central skills that manifest through discipline.

In **Chapter 3,** we examined the importance of focus and concentration. In today's fast-paced world, getting distracted and losing focus is typical. However, maintaining focus and attention is essential for achieving anything. It involves managing distractions, prioritizing tasks, and staying committed to your goals.

Focus and concentration must also be balanced with the ability to relax and rejuvenate. Taking breaks, engaging in activities you enjoy, and spending time with loved ones can help us recharge our batteries and return to work reinvigorated with renewed focus and energy.

In **Chapter 4,** you were shown the importance of work ethic. Success cannot be achieved overnight; it requires constant effort and the willingness to keep going, even when faced with setbacks and obstacles.

A solid work ethic encompasses the inner drive and determination to dedicate ample time and energy toward achieving your aspirations. It involves a deep-seated desire to do whatever is necessary to accomplish your goals and the readiness to persevere through challenging times. A strong work ethic demands a focused and unwavering commitment to consistently strive to progress and grow, leading to eventual success.

In **Chapter 5,** the importance of strategy and positioning was highlighted. Success is not just about working hard but also about working smart, so ensure you are doing both. A sound methodology involves leveraging your strengths and capabilities to your advantage.

It is necessary to integrate strategy and positioning with the ability to take risks. Sometimes, taking risks, stepping outside your comfort zone, and being open to innovative ideas and adept approaches yield the best opportunities.

In **Chapter 6,** we explored the importance of execution. Success is not just about having a good plan but also about taking action, which is essential for accomplishing anything.

One must incorporate reflection and self-evaluation with execution. We must take the time to analyze our progress, identify areas of improvement, and celebrate our accomplishments, which will help us stay motivated and focused on our goals.

In **Chapter 7,** we highlighted the importance of integrity. Integrity involves being honest and having unyielding moral principles. Integrity is essential for building trust and credibility and is the quintessential aspect of character development.

Integrity must be balanced with empathy and understanding. It is important to treat others with respect and compassion, even when you disagree with them or when they have different values or beliefs. Without integrity, success is hollow, and any achievement is meaningless.

In **Chapter 8,** we explored the concept of persistence. Success is not just about talent or intelligence but also about perseverance and resilience. Continuous execution is essential for success, especially when things get tough.

Persistence and resilience should be balanced with self-care and self-compassion by taking breaks, prioritizing relaxation, and cultivating a sense of self-compassion and self-acceptance for maximum results.

In **Chapter 9** of our journey, we examined the critical role of interdependence in attaining success. While individual achievements are significant, accomplishment is not limited to one person's efforts alone. Building strong relationships and collaborating with others is essential in today's world. Developing a supportive network of individuals who share common goals and aspirations is fundamental to success.

Effective communication and collaboration are crucial while working toward achieving shared objectives; building and managing these relationships can be challenging. Still, they provide a wealth of resources and knowledge that can help remove obstacles and lead to new opportunities. Interdependence offers a platform for mutual growth and achievement, paving the way for continued success in the future.

In **Chapter 10,** we explored the importance of energy, instinct, and intuition. While logical thinking and analyses are crucial, they alone cannot guarantee success. Success requires a comprehensive approach encompassing your intuition and spiritual intelligence.

Connecting with your inner self, trusting your instincts, and leveraging your intuition are all essential for making critical decisions and seizing opportunities. Listening to your inner voice and paying attention to your energy levels can help identify the most favorable paths.

Spiritual intelligence is about seeking meaning and purpose and aligning it with your goals and aspirations. It involves understanding your core values, beliefs, and motivations and using them to guide decisions that align with your overall purpose. You can access a deeper understanding of yourself and the world by tapping in, leading to greater clarity and direction.

Chapter 11 examined the significance of reflecting on your vision while remaining focused on your ultimate objective. While individual achievements are essential, true success is more than personal accomplishments. It involves positively impacting the world and leaving a lasting impression that inspires. Success consists of contributing to something greater than yourself and making a difference in the lives of others.

Reflecting on your existential contributions involves examining the impact you want to leave behind and the world you want to create for future generations. This process requires deep self-reflection and introspection. You can make a meaningful and lasting impact by aligning your actions with your purpose and core values, inspiring others to do the same. Striving to maintain ambitious standards and meaningfully influencing others both contribute to determining your lasting impact on the world.

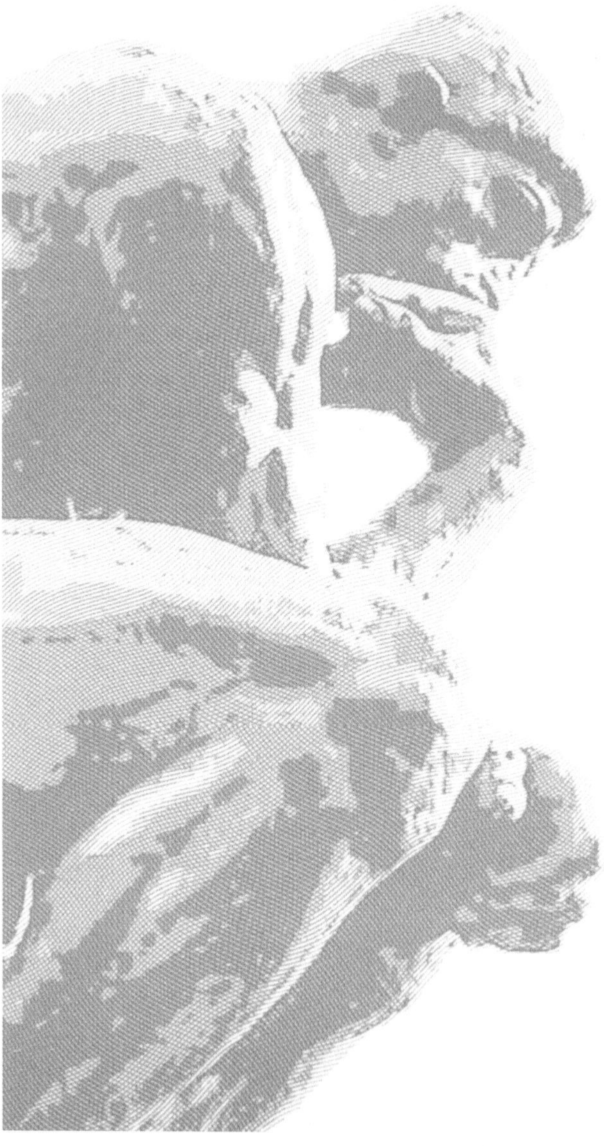

Synopsis

As you conclude this book, remember that success is more than achieving external goals and character development. A warrior mentality will help attain external success, but you must refine that mentality into adaptability, compassion, and determination.

"Only a life lived for others is a life worthwhile."
—Albert Einstein[36]

Defining success is not only about chasing dreams. Self-actualization and focusing on your purpose is the ultimate measure of success. Helping people, however altruistic, provides immeasurable fulfillment. It doesn't matter in which manner you choose to give back; it could be anything from charitable contributions to offering encouraging words to a listening ear or heavy heart. Our responsibility is to take care of one another. To navigate through life without doing so would be an abomination.

One must be willing to constantly improve, embrace change, and aspire to positively impact the world to ascend from a warrior mentality to a refined character. As you continue to move forward, stay relentless, remember the lessons covered in this volume, and strive to achieve success through fulfillment in all aspects of your life.

---

[36] Einstein Albert, "Only a Life Lived for Others Is a Life Worthwhile," Forbes Quotes, accessed September 24, 2023, https://www.forbes.com/quotes/192/.

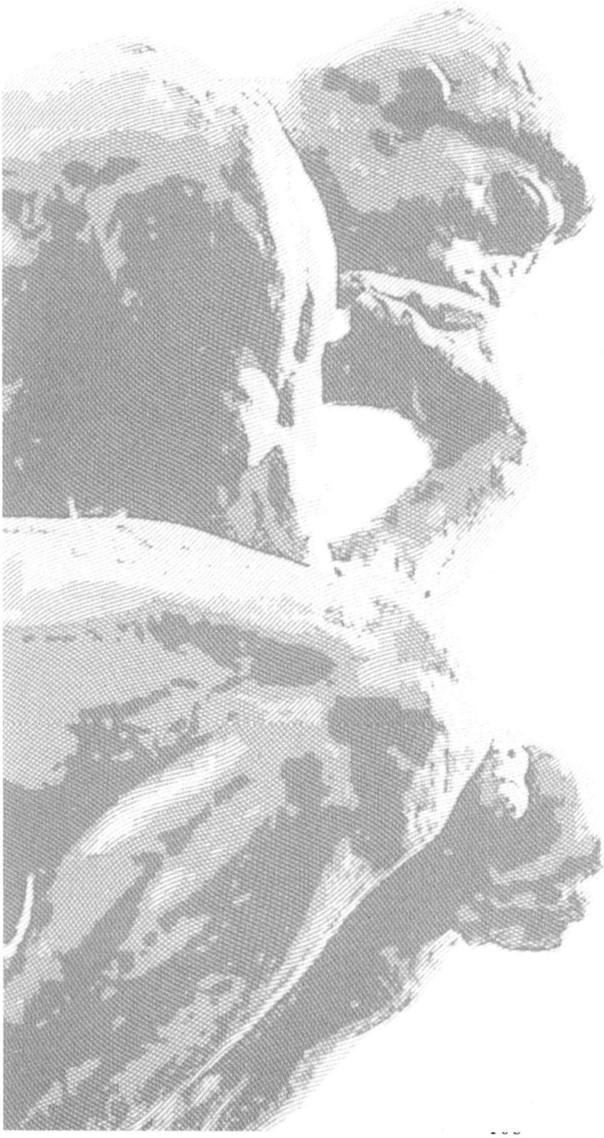

Acknowledgments

> "Either by kind words or supporting actions, the power of encouragement helps a person to rise on his feet and achieve his dreams."
>
> —Noora Ahmed Alsuwaidi

First and foremost, none of this would've been possible without the love and support of my family and friends. Even though I am in full ninja mode and invisible, all of you are in my heart, and I will never forget the sacrifices, love, support, and great memories.

To my loved ones who have transitioned and now live in the stars. May these words reach you. Your memory will live through the many lives you've impacted. You are in our hearts, and we will love you forever.

To my entire family, this book is more than a mere reflection of some of my thoughts, experiences, and achievements. The memories we created have helped shape the man I am today. Several family members contributed countless time, energy, and resources to ensure my immediate family was cared for. We are eternally grateful.

To my baby sister, who is my heart living outside my body, you are such a beautiful person, inside and out. You are the sweetest and most supportive person on the planet. You are a great mother! Thanks for always having my back. The world is a better place because of you. I love you!

To my father, who never stopped believing in me, thank you for the encouragement, support, and words of wisdom. I couldn't be prouder of you. Your devoted religious path, courage, and tenacity have inspired future generations. I am honored to be your son.

To my beautiful mother, your love, warrior spirit, and intellect were immeasurable. I can still feel your presence. Thank you for giving me life! We miss you more than words can express. May your memory live forever. I love you.

To my older sister, Deeca Miller-Lawrence, you are so much more than a sister. You sacrificed your childhood so that we could have a parent. You were more like a mother and became a great friend and my favorite person to travel with. Thanks for being by my side and for raising me right. Your emotions come from the depths of your soul, and my love for you is eternal.

To my "Big Brother," Donnie Shujah Miller (aka Shu), you have always been wise beyond your years. You are also one of the sharpest men on the planet; in appearance and thought. Your knowledge is incalculable. Thank you for being in my corner and for being such a great brother, leader, and powerful influence. I love you, Champ!

To my nieces and nephews, I love you more than you will ever know. You are all brilliant. The sky *isn't* the limit. There's nothing you can't do! I love you, believe in you, and am always available for you.

Uncle Harold Miller, aka Papa Harold, you took in an extra mouth to feed when you didn't have to. You were more than an uncle. You treated me as if I was your son. You taught me manners, respect, and much more, which has helped me to this day. I can still hear you singing that same song, "Have no fear...!" Thank you. – John Boy

To my Aunt Nancy Miller, a.k.a. Aunt Nunu, I remember the last time I saw you; you looked so happy with those thought-piercing eyes and beautiful smile. Thank you for giving me a place to stay, feeding and loving me. I remember you and Sharon showing up to every football and basketball game during my senior year. That type of support was foreign, and I will never forget it. I called you many late nights from Washington, DC, requesting assistance, and you came every time and brought food and money for my brother, sisters, and me. You are one of the people it is hard for me to think about because I love and miss you so much.

Aunt Brenda, Aunt Brenda, Aunt Brenda. Every moment with you was brief, however monumental. You couldn't have been any sweeter. Your superpower was making everyone you encountered feel like they were on top of the world. Hopefully, you and my mother will read this together. I love and miss you both.

To my beautiful cousin, Sharon Chalmers-Hill, your heart is a diamond. You are so strong and brilliant. I have so many things to thank you for. The world is a better place because of you. Thank you for giving me a place to stay, feeding, and constantly encouraging me. I remember many years; Christmas and my birthday would have been disappointing occasions without you and Aunt Nunu. Thanks for being my friend and thank you for loving me.

To my Aunt Kathleen Smith, thank you for the tough love, for keeping me fed, and for giving me a place to stay for a little while. Thanks for keeping me on track. I remember the many heartfelt discussions where you sat me down and made me carefully consider the impact and consequences of my behavior and decisions on my life. May your memory live forever. You were a blessing to this world!

To Alexandria Strielkauskas, RN (aka Lexi), you are one of the sweetest people on the planet. Your heart is bigger than your body. It is fascinating how you don't let anything or anybody stand in your way. Keep it up! I'm proud of you; I feel honored that we met. I will forever be in your corner. You deserve every blessing that you receive. Thank you for being so supportive. I love you for that! And thank you for loving me. – Covie P.

Aunt Joyce, you have always gone above and beyond to be the glue that held the family together. You kept a full house and an open door, and it didn't matter whose kids they were. Thank you for always being there for my siblings and me. You did more for us than we could ever imagine. I love you for that!

A huge and heartfelt thank you to Mrs. Diane Page and family. You were like a mother to me. Thank you so much for taking me in, no questions asked, treating me like one of your own, and loving me. You touched so many hearts, especially mine! You changed my life. Your memory will echo for eternity.

To my brother Mark Goins, aka Smoke, thanks for believing in me to an exponential degree. Your actions far exceed your words. I would go to war with you any day. You are one of the most dependable and consistent people on the planet. Out of everyone I know, you are the one person I would call if my life depended on you showing up, and I love you for that. You are a great brother and a loyal friend. Sha – From the Outer Upper Realm

Perry McIver, your hard work, and drive are an inspiration to many. You never complain; you just handle your business. Congratulations on your success; you deserve it! You are also one of the most dependable people on the planet, and I appreciate your friendship and support. Thank you for being such a great brother and friend. Your mother was an angel.

Kendall Chalmers-Wrencher, how your eyes light up when I see you is worth a million words. Your energy is powerful. Thank you for being so loving and supportive. You watched me grow and mature, and our conversation followed suit. It's always a pleasure talking to you. You don't match energy; you <u>elevate</u> whoever you come in contact with. I love you!

Garrett Chalmers (aka G), - You're my cousin and friend, but we are more like brothers. You willingly did so much for me. You helped me mature. When you speak, right or wrong, it's always direct, genuine, full of wisdom, and from the heart. Thanks for always being in my corner. I love you, Champ!

To my cousin Denene Chalmers. If I ever needed anything, I could always count on you. That's something I will never forget. Thanks for the many late-night rides and encouraging conversations. Thanks for feeding me, and thanks for loving me. I love you.

To my charismatic cousin Johnsie Gaddy, it's always an honor to be in your presence. I have never seen you without a smile. Your conversation is empowering and full of wisdom. Thank you for showing me love from day one. You couldn't be more special. I love you, and I love your energy.

Mrs. Mary McLaughlin (Grandma), you told me I was one of yours, and that's exactly how you treated me and made me feel. You told me to stay sweet, which seemed simple but has proven challenging, but I will continue, as promised. I miss your hugs and your sweet voice. May your memory live forever through your legacy. I love you, Grandma.

Senior Master Sergeant Anthony Dupree, USAF, Retired, I am honored to be your brother. You moved a few mountains for me; I appreciate it and will continue to pay it forward. They say, "God gives his toughest battles to his strongest soldiers." With that said, what does that make you? Exactly! Keep it up and continue to lead by example.

Warren and Cherita Weems, you two are royalty and truly an inspiration. You welcomed me into your life with love and opened my eyes to a world I didn't know existed. You are two of the most genuine and loving people I've ever met. Thanks for the realness, and thanks for feeding and loving me. I love you both. #JYB4Life

My brother, William Van Lawrence, aka Billy Boots, you are a warrior. Even cancer was no match! Let them watch you while you stand on the speakers and motivate. Your mother is still with you in everything that you do. Keep going hard in her memory! You are larger than life. Much love – Brick

To my beautiful Aunt Mae, I think you might be an angel. You have a powerful light around you. Not only reflective in words but the consistency of your actions. I will never forget how you stopped the world from spinning for me when I recently moved back to D.C. I love you.

To Mrs. Michelle, Danny Stewart, and your entire beautiful family of amazing people, from the first day we met, you welcomed me into your home and your family with open arms and that's something I will never forget. I love you both, and I love your entire family. Thanks for loving me.

Ms. Linda Goins, thank you for the love and thanks for feeding me. I miss your energy, and I miss our talks. You left this world entirely too soon. You are loved and missed. May your memory live forever.

Sandra Webb, aka Sandy, you are brilliant, and I'm not just saying that to get free sweet-potato cupcakes. Thank you for the love, wisdom, and support. I love your drive. Your positive energy is a breath of fresh air. I'm honored to know the real you. I love you.

Yolanda Chavis, thank you for the love and encouragement. You are a great friend and I'm blessed to have you. Your ambition speaks louder than your words, which is how it should be in life and business. Keep going hard and congratulations on your success. Stop at nothing. I love you.

Gerard Anthony (W56), your energy is very powerful. Your work ethic couldn't be more impressive! Thanks for giving me the keys to the castle. If I needed anything, you were there, no questions asked, and I will never forget that. I love you and your family. "All The Way...!" – B52

Thank you to my brother, Master Sergeant Lorenzo White (aka Zoe), USAF, Retired, and my brilliant sister, Kita White, PhD; you two were always there for me, no matter what. I could call at 3 a.m. without notice, and you willingly laid out the red carpet for me. You two have the best energy. Your daughter took my heart and never gave it back. I love your whole family.

Senior Chief Petty Officer Otis Frazier, USN, Retired; from day one, we were brothers. Thanks for being in my corner and for the genuine love and loyalty. I couldn't be prouder of you! This is only the beginning of your empire that you are building with Shazzy! Stop at nothing! Proverbs 27:17. I love you – Kinfolk

To my brother, Master Sergeant John Kennedy, USAF, Retired, first of all, everything you touch seems to flourish. You've got the Midas touch; it's just something to think about. We have been through more things than I care to recall, and what may seem like near-death experiences were blessings in disguise. Look at us now. You are destined for greatness. Keep it up! I'm proud of you, Jay. I love you and your family.

Dewitt Russell (aka Big Russ), thank you for the encouragement and support. You have some of the best ideas on the planet! You will become unstoppable once you understand your power and focus on that and nothing else. Control your influences. Control your energy. Control your life! Go hard now and forever. No prisoners! #MDR

Calvin Watford, Esq., I appreciate you and Star for being in my corner. Congratulations on passing the bar. Your work ethic, discipline, and focus got the job done. I'm proud of you. Stop at nothing. Brick

To Asif Nadeem, thank you for your hard work and dedication to all of our projects; both current and imminent. You have consistently proven to be much more than a seller or provider of a service. You are my friend, my brother, and my most valuable team member. Every task or project that we work on together evolves into a masterpiece. I would not be where I am today without GOD, the encouragement of my family and friends, and your keen sense of direction, creativity, and unprecedented ability to manage and execute.

Alfonso Knight, you are one of the best to ever do it. You take care of so many people and do it without hesitation. There's nothing you can't do. Keep dreaming BIG. Like I told you before, nobody is better than you. I'm in your corner. Thanks for the realness. D2G4Life – Unk

Chief Master Sergeant Ashley (aka Big Swol), USAF, Retired. You took me under your wing as your younger brother and helped me prepare for my first bodybuilding competition. I quickly realized that I wasn't only training my body; everything we did was to sharpen my mind. There is nothing I can't do, and I owe the advent of that understanding to you for challenging me. I love you for that. I never had the opportunity to thank you. I will make sure you receive this book in person.

Coach André and Courtney Brunson, thank you for welcoming me to college and making me part of your family. I never took the opportunity to let you know what a profound impact you two had on me, but being with your family was by far one of my most memorable experiences at Tuskegee. I will always consider you family. I love you both. – Brick

I wish to thank General Steven R. Lyons, US Army, Retired. You are one of the greatest leaders I have ever had the honor to work with. I learned a great deal from your leadership style: courage, focus, discipline, and commitment. Even today, I reflect on your example for guidance.

Finally, a special shout-out to all those who were a part of my journey:
Ajul and Janice Jones
Ali Cummings
Anthony Blue
Anthony Crockett
Antwan and Larette Wallace
Antwan Blue
Antwan Lewis and Family
Archie Aples
Bimini Heard and Family
Bo Chalmers
Brian Cavanaugh
Brian Fluellen
Brian Rampy and Family
Brian Strictland
Calvin Watford, Esq., Star, and Family
Caprice Coleman
CAPT Brain Hinkley, USN, Retired
Carlton Core
Cathy Kennedy
Charlene Ingram and Family
Charles McLaughlin
Charles Nketia and Family
Chris Peterkin
Chris Wilson
Claudia Lantz
Coach McArthur Shivers
Conrad Wrencher
CPO Nicholas Mosley
Dale Baker
Darlene Phillips
David Chestnut
David Lewis
David McKenzie
David Shaw and Family
Debra Frye and Family
Derrick Malloy
Derrick McKayhan

Dina Wade
Donise Holley
Dot Smith and Family
Dr. Benjamin Greene
Dr. Christa Pettie
Dr. Ronikka C. Hannans
Drake Murphy and Family
Efren Gatan
Enzo Nabiev, Esq.
Eneshal Miller
Eric Sexton
Ernest Calhoun
Ernest Jacobs and Family
Gabe Lockhart
Gloria and Mike
GOD
Godfrey Wilson
Greg Allbrooks and Family
Greg Hainsworth and Family
Hasheem Chalmers
Henry Douglas and Family
J. Antar Campbell
Jaime Boggan and Family
Jamil Miller
Jane Duke
Jim and Marilyn Russell
Jonathan McLaren
Juanessa Lucas
Keith Utley
Kenny Acob
Kim Wade and Family
Kristi Pope
Latoya Waddell
Lavita Critchlow
Lawrence Joseph Lovato
Lessie Moore
Liling Cavanaugh
Linda Smith and Family

Linnell Hart
Lisa Thomas
Mani Pathak
Marcus Gillis
Marianna and De'Angelo
Marisha Chalmers
Marketa Council and Family
Marlon Chalmers
Marwaan Miller
MCPO Timothy Sheridan, Retired
MGySgt Sean McRae, Retired
Michael Spear
Mika Thompson
Mike Lockwood and Family
Mike Ly
Mike Stein
Milton Hill
My Bothers-in-Arms
My Brother Drew
My Brother Sport and Family
Nancy Evans
Nathaniel Brown
Neya Dowling
Omar and Tatjana Pilgrim
Pat Ward
Randall Williams
Raqqi Chalmers
Regina Palmer and Family
Regina Washington
Reginal Fields
Robert Ingram
Robert Roberson and Family
Rose Baldwin
Sam Waters
Sandra Webb
Sean McGuigan
Seth and Ahlia Ray
Shane Page

Shayla Smith
Shirley Mason and Family
Stephen and Paige Johnson
Steven "Moe" Williams
Tastie Ewing
Tequan Chalmers
Terry Bailey
Terry Barnes
Terri Williams
Terrance and Patrina Fuller
Tessie Taylor and Family
The 82nd Airborne Division
The Allbrooks Family
The Bacon Family
The Cagle Family
The Dirty Dozen
The Lawyer Family
The Strielkauskas Family
Titania Jacobs and Family
Torrance Heggie
Travis Baker
Tremaine McLeod
Tuskegee University
Tyrone Jackson
Uncle Abu Muhammad Saleem
Uncle Bruce and Jerry Reaves
Uncle Freddie Miller
Uncle Joe Jackson
Uncle Redell Miller
Vernell Powell
Veronica Swinson

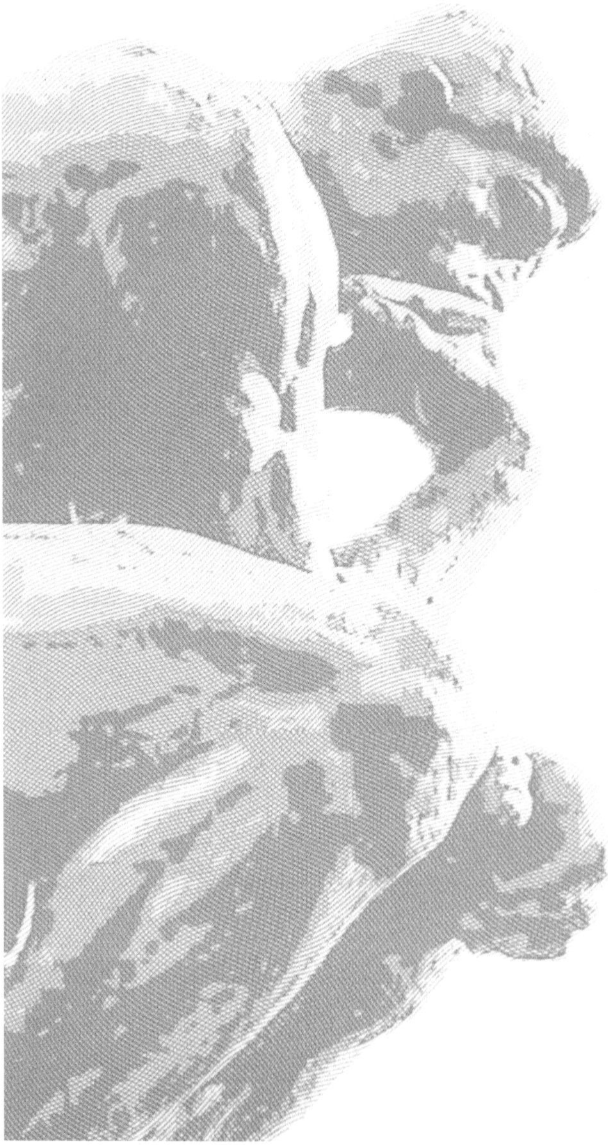

ABOUT THE AUTHOR

Meet Johnny Miller

Johnny Miller is a remarkable man with numerous talents that have propelled him to success in business and beyond as a motivational speaker, author, and business owner.

Johnny owns the motivational clothing brand Wakeup Kill Sh*t Repeat, which he has successfully run for over five years. His team creates rugged athletic apparel tailored to a highly active consumer demographic while ensuring the company's message of relentless optimism and perseverance is reflected throughout the brand.

Before launching his successful businesses, he managed problems, implemented strategic solutions, and resolved long-standing issues for the US Department of State as an Emergency Communications Officer. His rewarding yet challenging position enabled him to refine critical thinking skills that he continues to master.

Through his actions, Johnny effectively communicates the significance of resilience, taking action, and embracing change as opportunities for growth. He approaches challenges like a skilled tactician—detailed, calculated, methodical, yet persevering. His experience, grit, and mental toughness make him one of the most resilient individuals on the planet, recognized by the Guinness World Records association for the most weight ever lifted by bicep curls in one minute as of December 17, 2022.

Driven by purpose, Johnny leverages his platform as a motivational speaker to inspire others to take action, irrespective of influence and external factors.

Johnny Miller was born and raised in Washington, DC, and Southern Pines, North Carolina. Serving at Air Force bases Langley in Virginia and Kadena in Japan, his exceptional performance earned him recognition as Top Performer of the Year. Inspired by his life journey, he authored the book *How Did You Get So Brave?* and had a role in the movie *The Ties That Bind*.

In his leisure time, Johnny enjoys peace of mind, hardcore sweat-inducing workouts, playing chess, and cherished moments of relaxation with his beloved father.

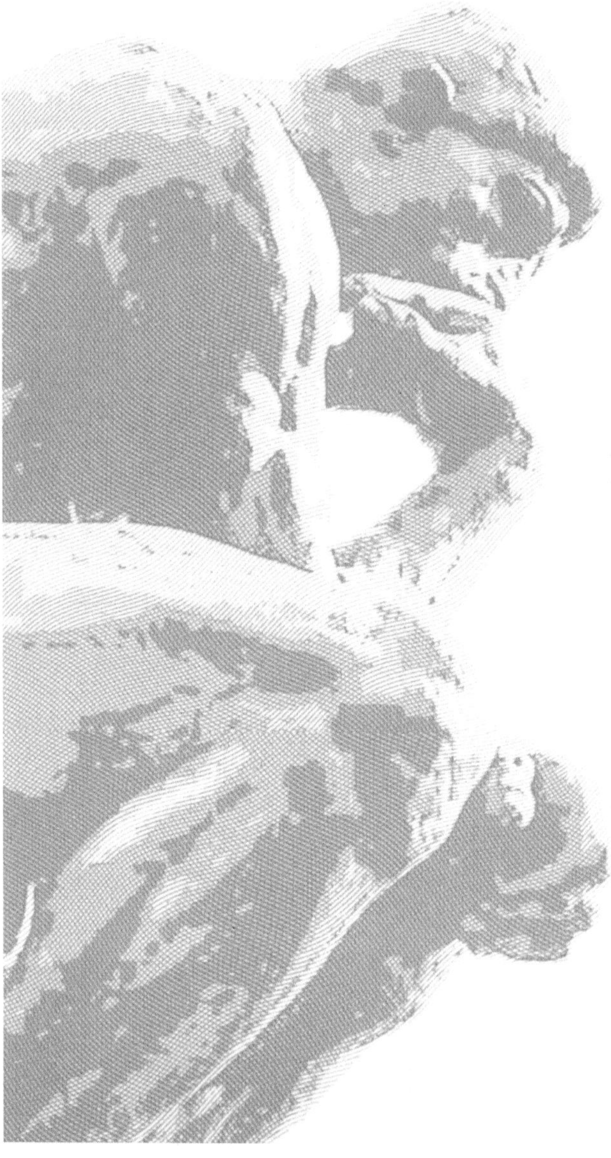

BIBLIOGRAPHY

Alaili, Abdallah. "If You Really Look Closely, Most Overnight Successes Took a Long Time. – Steve Jobs. Entrepreneur Post, November 11, 2020. https://www.entrepreneurpost.com/2020/11/11/if-you-really-look-closely-most-overnight-successes-took-a-long-time-steve-jobs/

Ashe, Arthur. "Success Is a Journey, not a Destination. The Doing Is Often More Important Than the Outcome." BrainyQuote. Accessed September 24, 2023. https://www.brainyquote.com/quotes/arthur_ashe_371528

Austin, Ryan. "Top 10 Jay-Z Quotes About Success." Deeper Freedom (blog). Accessed September 23, 2023. https://deeperfreedom.com/jay-z-quotes-about-success/

Bodhipaksa. "Publilius Syrus, "To Do Two Things at Once Is to Do Neither."" Wildmind, February 23, 2009. https://www.wildmind.org/blogs/quote-of-the-month/publilius-syrus

Brown, Paul B. "'You Miss 100% of the Shots You Don't Take.' You Need to Start Shooting at Your Goals." Forbes, January 12, 2014. https://www.forbes.com/sites/actiontrumpseverything/2014/01/12/you-miss-100-of-the-shots-you-dont-take-so-start-shooting-at-your-goal/?sh=26629b116a40

Buck, Pearl S. "The Young Do Not Know Enough to Be Prudent, and Therefore They Attempt the Impossible - and Achieve It, Generation After Generation." BrainyQuote. Accessed September 23, 2023. https://www.brainyquote.com/quotes/pearl_s_buck_161681

Burns, George. "I Look to the Future Because That's Where I'm Going to Spend the Rest of My Life." BrainyQuote. Accessed September 24, 2023. https://www.brainyquote.com/quotes/george_burns_189717

Buxton, Charles. "You Will Never Find Time for Anything. If You Want Time, You Must Make It." BrainyQuote. Accessed September 23, 2023. https://www.brainyquote.com/quotes/charles_buxton_104418

Cuban, Mark. "Work Like There Is Someone Working Twenty-Four Hours a Day to Take It All Away from You." Quotefancy. Accessed September 23, 2023. https://quotefancy.com/quote/1151819/Mark-Cuban-Work-like-there-is-someone-working-twenty-four-hours-a-day-to-take-it-all-away

Edison, Thomas. "Our Greatest Weakness Lies in Giving up. The Most Certain Way to Succeed Is Always to Try Just One More Time." BrainyQuote. Accessed September 23, 2023. https://www.brainyquote.com/quotes/thomas_a_edison_149049

Einstein Albert. "Only a Life Lived for Others Is a Life Worthwhile." Forbes Quotes. Accessed September 24, 2023. https://www.forbes.com/quotes/192/

Franklin, Benjamin. "You May Delay, but Time Will Not." BrainyQuote. Accessed September 23, 2023. https://www.brainyquote.com/quotes/benjamin_franklin_101831

Gorky, Maxim. "The Higher Goal a Person Pursues, the Quicker His Ability Develops, and the More Beneficial He Will Become to the Society…." Quotefancy. Accessed September 24, 2023. https://quotefancy.com/quote/1057713/Maxim-Gorky-The-higher-goal-a-person-pursues-the-quicker-his-ability-develops-and-the

Heather. "Excuses Will Always Be There for You. Opportunity Won't." Mindset Made Better, November 28, 2022. Accessed September 23, 2023. https://mindsetmadebetter.com/2022/11/excuses-will-always-be-there-for-you-opportunity-wont/

Hidy, Lynn. "To Finish First, You Must First Finish." Inside Sales Leadership Corner (blog), Up Your Telesales, June 7, 2021. https://www.upyourtelesales.com/2021/06/07/to-finish-first-you-must-first-finish/

Hormozi, Alex. "You Don't Become Confident by Shouting Affirmations in the Mirror, but by Having a Stack of Undeniable Proof That You Are Who You Say You Are. Outwork Your Self Doubt." Twitter, October 29, 2022, 12:34 pm. Accessed September 23, 2023.
https://twitter.com/AlexHormozi/status/1586441477952921600

Hubbard, Elbert. "The World Is Moving So Fast These Days That the Man Who Says It Can't Be Done Is Generally Interrupted by Someone Doing It." BrainyQuote. Accessed September 23, 2023.
https://www.brainyquote.com/quotes/elbert_hubbard_131125

Hubbard, Elbert. Little Journeys to the Homes of American Statesmen. 1898. Reprinted. New York: The Knickerbocker Press, 1901.
http://hdl.handle.net/2027/hvd.hx4zk6

Huntsman, Jon M. Winners Never Cheat: Even in Difficult Times. Revised edition. Upper Saddle River, New Jersey: Pearson Education, 2014.
https://ptgmedia.pearsoncmg.com/images/9780137009039/samplepages/9780137009039.pdf

Jefferson, Thomas. "In Matters of Style, Swim with the Current; in Matters of Principle, Stand Like a Rock." BrainyQuote. Accessed September 23, 2023.
https://www.brainyquote.com/quotes/thomas_jefferson_121032

Jordan, Michael. "It's Not How Hard You Pushed Along the Way. It's Having Something in You to Finish." Quotefancy. Accessed September 24, 2023.
https://quotefancy.com/quote/867570/Michael-Jordan-It-s-not-how-hard-you-pushed-along-the-way-It-s-having-something-in-you-to

Kerr, James. "5 Reasons True Leadership Is All About Character." Inc., February 1, 2016. https://www.inc.com/james-kerr/leadership-in-a-nutshell.html

Lama, Dalai. "There Are Only Two Days in the Year That Nothing Can Be Done. One Is Called Yesterday and the Other Is Called Tomorrow." Minimalist Quotes. Accessed September 23, 2023. https://minimalistquotes.com/dalai-lama-quote-8442/

Leibowitz, Pamela. ""There Are No Secrets to Success. It Is the Result of Preparation, Hard Work, and Learning from Failure."- Colin Powell." Suffolk Center for Speech. Accessed September 23, 2023.
https://www.lispeech.com/there-are-no-secrets-to-success-it-is-the-result-of-preparation-hard-work-and-learning-from-failure-colin-powell/

Loftus, Geoff. "If You're Going Through Hell, Keep Going - Winston Churchill." Forbes, May 9, 2012. https://www.forbes.com/sites/geoffloftus/2012/05/09/if-youre-going-through-hell-keep-going-winston-churchill/?sh=29db1498d549

Loken, Petter. "Lessons from Steve Jobs." January 6, 2021. Accessed September 23, 2023. https://www.petterloken.no/post/lessons-from-steve-jobs

Marouf, Moneer. "Obsidian Studio Announces Edyn, an Action Adventure Game Taking Place in a Vibrant Immersive World." EIN Presswire, February 7, 2022. https://www.einnews.com/pr_news/562507694/obsidian-studio-announces-edyn-an-action-adventure-game-taking-place-in-a-vibrant-immersive-world

Megginson, Leon C. "Lessons from Europe for American Business." The Southwestern Social Science Quarterly 44, no. 1 (1963): 3–13. http://www.jstor.org/stable/42866937

Merton, Sophia. ""We Are What We Repeatedly Do" - Meaning and History - Stoic Quotes." StoicQuotes.com, February 28, 2023. https://stoicquotes.com/we-are-what-we-repeatedly-do/

Murphy, Andy. "A Reason to Stay Away from Negative People (According to Albert Einstein)." Medium, July 19, 2022. https://medium.com/writers-blokke/a-reason-to-stay-away-from-negative-people-according-to-albert-einstein-9139189166a

Newton, Isaac. "If I Have Seen Further Than Others, It Is by Standing Upon the Shoulders of Giants." BrainyQuote. Accessed September 24, 2023. https://www.brainyquote.com/quotes/isaac_newton_135885

Shah, Meet. "Winning Isn't Everything, but Wanting to Win Is." Setquotes, August 14, 2022. https://www.setquotes.com/winning-isnt-everything-but-wanting-to-win-is/

Stanford. "Steve Jobs' 2005 Stanford Commencement Address." YouTube, March 7, 2008, video, 15:04. https://youtu.be/UF8uR6Z6KLc?si=_UV7lemCgWsHdMWN

Stoner, Kayla. "Science Proves That What Doesn't Kill You Makes You Stronger." Northwestern University, October 1, 2019.

https://news.northwestern.edu/stories/2019/10/science-proves-that-what-doesnt-kill-you-makes-you-stronger/

Washington, Booker T. "Success Is to Be Measured Not So Much by the Position That One Has Reached in Life as by the Obstacles Which He Has Overcome." BrainyQuote. Accessed September 23, 2023. https://www.brainyquote.com/quotes/booker_t_washington_107996

Winfrey, Oprah. "You Become What You Believe. You Are Where You Are Today in Your Life Based on Everything You Have Believed." Quotefancy. Accessed September 23, 2023. https://quotefancy.com/quote/879511/Oprah-Winfrey-You-become-what-you-believe-You-are-where-you-are-today-in-your-life-based

Wooden, John. "If You Don't Have Time to Do It Right, When Will You Have Time to Do It Over?" BrainyQuote. Accessed September 23, 2023. https://www.brainyquote.com/quotes/john_wooden_384653

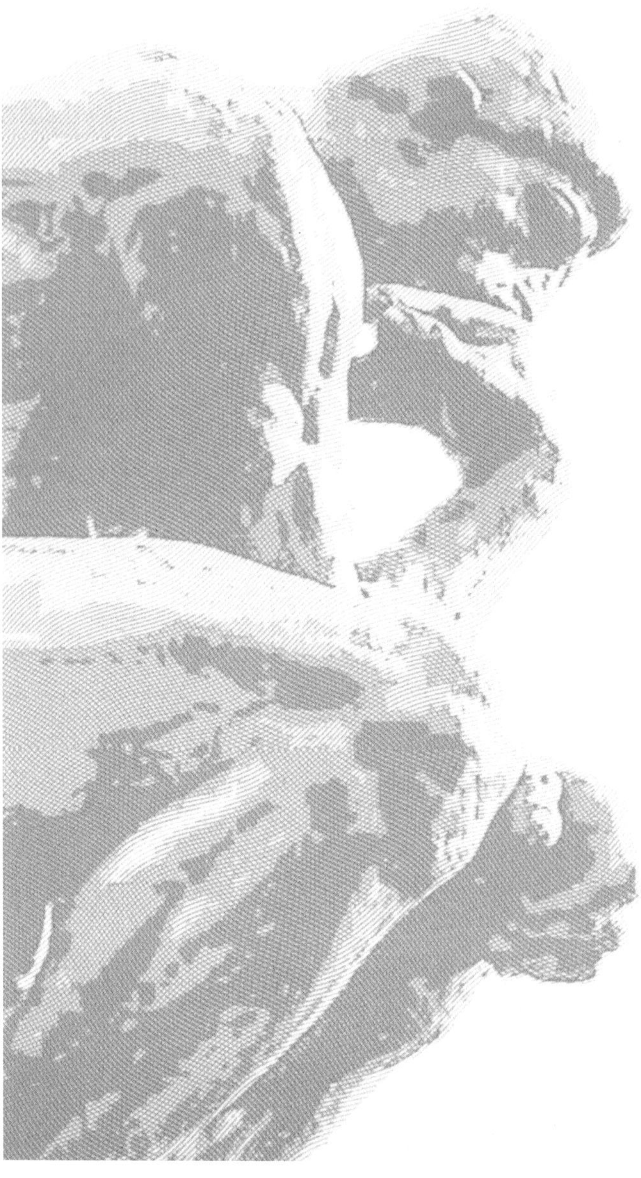

INDEX

Abundance mindset, 101
Accountability, 69
Action plan, 53
Adversity, 7, 16, 71
Advertising, 80
Affirmations, 41
Alsuwaidi. Noora Ahmed, 109
Ambition
   Lack of, 32
Analytical complexity, 53
Assistance, 45, 80, 111
Attention engineering, 33
Autonomous forces, 77
Awareness, 11, 56, 87
Beliefs, 87, 103, 104
Boundaries, 24
Brainstorming, 23, 50, 61
Buck, Pearl S., 60, 127
Burnout, 101
Burns, George, 93, 128
Buxton, Charles, 21
Capability, 4, 42, 47
Challenges, 9, 31, 34, 100, 124
Character development, 103
Churchill, Winston, 56, 130
Collaboration, 104
Comfort zone, 49
Commitment, 102, 116
Communication, 80
Community, 75
Compassion, 64, 103
Completion date, 23, 63
Concentration, 35, 68, 102
Confidence, 4, 9, 59, 101

Confirmation bias, 84
Conscious thoughts, 89
Consistency, 101
Constant effort, 27, 38, 57, 100
Core values, 104
Courage, 16, 83, 96, 110, 116
Credibility, 67, 103
Cuban, Mark, 9
Dalai Lama, 22
Delayed gratification, 42
Dermographism urticaria, 11
Determination, 4, 59, 96, 102
Discernment, 90
Discipline, 4, 33, 36, 45, 99, 101, 102, 116
   Consistency, 27
   Developing, 4
Disparity, 79
Distractions, 29, 33, 96
Dopamine, 13
Durant, Will, 49
Edison, Thomas, 18
Effective communication, 104
Efficiency, 53
Einstein, Albert, 84, 107, 128, 130
Emotional intelligence, 80
Emotions, 10, 89
Empathy, 103
Excuses, 9, 42, 49, 73
Failure, 22, 80
Fangio, Juan Manuel, 97
Fear of failure, 16, 59
Fearless warrior, 16
Financial advice, 45

Financial plan, 45
Flexibility, 34
Franklin, Benjamin, 59, 128
Fulfillment, 100
Future generations, 110
Goals, 17, 64, 99, 100, 104
    Commitment, 15
    Execution, 61
    Focus and concentration, 29, 34
    Persistence, 72
    Prioritizing, 4
    Self-Control, 27
    Short-term, 26
    Strategy, 53
    Work ethic, 49, 50
Gorky, Maksim, 71, 128
Gratitude, 8, 101
Gretzky, Wayne, 60
Growth mindset, 79
Growth opportunities, 33
Habits, 42
    Habits, 23
Hormozi, Alex, 41
Hubbard, Elbert, 4, 68
Huntsman Sr, Jon, 100
Indecisiveness, 16
Inner strength, 4
Innovative ideas, 79
Inspiration, 112
Instincts, 83, 99, 104
Integrity
    Definition, 69
    Personal, 64
    Refined character, 99, 103
    Trust and credibility, 67
Interdependence, 77, 99, 103
Intuition, 83, 84, 89, 99, 104
    Spiritual, 89
    Trusting, 89, 90
Jefferson, Thomas, 67

Jobs, Steve, 45, 83, 127, 130
Jordan, Michael, 80, 95, 129
Karma, 89
Laser-like focus, 23, 33, 69
Learning from failure, 22
Lee, Bruce, 10
Leveraged resources, 80
Lombardi, Vince, 14
Long-term gains, 102
Marine Corps, 35, 36
Megginson, Leon C, 53, 130
Mental clarity, 33, 83
Mental fortitude, 11
Metaphysical, 89
Methodology, 102
Mindset
    Current, 11
    Right, 33
Money, 44, 45, 68, 96, 111
    Focus and concentration, 33, 34
    Integrity, 68
    Making, 96
    Strategy, 56
    Warrior mentality, 13
Moral principles, 103
Motivation, 13, 32, 45, 63, 69, 83, 91, 99, 101, 104
Motivational speaker, 123, 124
Negative influences, 32
Negative people, 84
Negative thinking, 60
Newton, Isaac, 77, 130
Nietzsche, Friedrich, 7
Objectives, 24, 77, 78, 91, 101, 104
Obstacles, 24, 41, 57, 72, 102, 104
Opportunity, 9, 19, 61, 73, 115, 128
Optimism, 8, 123
Overanalyzing, 60
Overthinking, 59
Persistence, 99, 103

Personal achievement, 34
Planning, 96
Primary objective, 73
Priorities, 59, 64
Pro Football, 36
Procrastination, 16, 60
Productivity, 18, 32, 77
Progress, 19, 61, 62, 64, 73, 96, 101, 102
Psychological manipulation, 91
Purpose, 11, 33, 36, 45, 48, 96, 101, 104, 124
Quantum realm, 89
Relationships, 68, 74, 89, 100, 103, 104
Research, 32, 48, 89
Resilience, 103, 124
Resource selection, 53
Rigid flexibility, 34, 78
Roles and responsibilities, 79
Routine, 23, 24, 34, 62
Sacrifices, 21, 36, 95, 102, 109
Schwarzkopf, Norman, 99
Seconds in a day, 19, 46
Self-care, 103
Self-control, 24, 47, 102
Self-esteem, 32
Self-improvement, 99
Setbacks, 41, 102
Spiritual intelligence, 104
Spirituality, 87, 99
Strategy, 46, 50, 53, 55, 60, 93, 94, 99, 102
Strengths, 75, 77, 99, 102
Subconscious mind, 42
Success, 4, 18, 22, 23, 49, 99, 100, 101, 102, 103, 104, 123
  Long-term, 21
Synchronicities, 89
Syrus, Publius, 29
Task prioritization, 53
Transcendental, 89
Trojan horse, 33
Ultimate objective, 104
Values, 103
Warrior mentality, 101
Warrior spirit, 110
Watford, Calvin, 17
Weaknesses, 77, 99
Willpower, 11, 42, 59
Winfrey, Oprah, 34
Wooden, John, 43
Work ethic, 99, 102
Work-life balance, 101